To Jerry and ELIZABETH —
THANK YOU FOR coming To
My NAPA TALK —
Best Calmus
Ava F. Karl

Jewish
Life
in the
American
West

Jewish Life

in the American West

PERSPECTIVES ON MIGRATION, SETTLEMENT, AND COMMUNITY

Edited by
Ava F. Kahn

AUTRY MUSEUM OF WESTERN HERITAGE
Los Angeles

in association with

UNIVERSITY OF WASHINGTON PRESS
Seattle and London

To Pearl Salzberg, whose intellectual curiosity

inspires me every day

—Ava F. Kahn

This book was published in conjunction with the exhibition *Jewish Life in the American West: Generation to Generation*, organized by the Autry Museum of Western Heritage and held there from June 21, 2002, through January 20, 2003.

Library of Congress Cataloging-in-Publication Data

Jewish life in the American West : perspectives on migration,
settlement, and community / edited by Ava F. Kahn.
    p. cm.
Published in conjunction with an exhibition organized by the Autry
Museum of Western Heritage and held there June 21, 2002-January 20, 2003.
  ISBN 0-295-98275-6 (Paperback : alk. paper)
  1. Jews—West (U.S.)—History—Exhibitions. 2.
Jews—Migrations—Exhibitions. 3. West (U.S.)—Emigration and
immigration—Exhibitions. 4. Immigrants—West (U.S.)—History—19th
century—Exhibitions. 5. Immigrants—West (U.S.)—History—20th
century—Exhibitions. I. Kahn, Ava Fran. II. Autry Museum of Western
Heritage.
  F596.3.J5 J47 2002
  973.04924—dc21

                2002005002

The paper used in this publication is acid free and recycled from ten percent postconsumer and at least fifty percent preconsumer waste. It meets the minimum requirements of American National Standard for Information Sciences—Permanence of Paper for Printed Materials, ANSI Z39.48–1984.

Designed by Dana Levy, Perpetua Press
Printed in Hong Kong by Toppan Printing Co.

COVER: Jewish Hungarian immigrants Adolph and Sam Frankel, c. 1920, in Cushing, Oklahoma. Photo from Allen and Cynthia Salzman Mondell's documentary film *West of Hester Street*.

BACK COVER: The Newmark family in Yosemite, 1884. From the Archives of *Western States Jewish History*.

Contents

7   Foreword
        James H. Nottage

13   Introduction: Looking at America from the West to the East, 1850–1920s
        Ava F. Kahn

33   American West, New York Jewish
        Hasia R. Diner

53   To Journey West: Jewish Women and Their Pioneer Stories
        Ava F. Kahn

83   The Jewish Merchant and Civic Order in the Urban West
        William Toll

113   From Cooperative Farming to Urban Leadership
        Ellen Eisenberg

133   Afterword
        Moses Rischin

138   Selected Readings

140   Acknowledgments

141   Index

HOMINY'S FAMOUS JEWISH CHAMPION

OF THE LARIAT & SADDLE

Foreword

James H. Nottage

JUST WHAT IS A WESTERNER? Cowboys and Indians populate the West in the minds of many. With the influence of such popular media as film and television, this view of sharp-toed boots and feathered headdresses is continually endorsed. Of course, trappers, troopers, merchants, train men, schoolteachers, and many others also come to mind in stereotyping the citizens of the frontier. So, is a westerner defined by occupation? Or is a westerner someone who just does western things such as roping, riding, and ranching? Is a westerner simply somebody who looks to be of and from the region by virtue of how he or she dresses? Do these ideas then exclude from the ranks of westerners urban dwellers in Denver, Houston, or San Francisco who dress in fashions reflecting trends of the East?

There is, indeed, a singular set of perceptions that comes to mind when most individuals give thought to the historical peopling of the American West. Perhaps this is one of the major reasons that until recent years comparatively little attention has been paid to the real diversity of these populations. Fortunately, earlier generations' views of the region are changing as ideas of gender, ethnicity, age, national origin, and belief are being carefully explored by new generations of historians and are even being addressed in mythical treatments of the region.

Jewish immigrants played a wide variety of roles in the history of the West, even as cowboys and Indians! Any number of Jewish ranchers and cowboys can be named, and Solomon Bibo married into the family of an

"Hominy's famous Jewish champion of the lariat & saddle." Courtesy of High Noon Collectibles, Los Angeles.

Acoma Pueblo leader and himself became leader of the community. Jewish people were an integral part of the western story, and the West is an integral part of the increasingly recognized and better understood American Jewish experience.

Of course, every population drawn together by common origin or belief is usually diverse itself. This is no less true for Jews who came from different countries of the world, including Germany, France, Hungary, Russia, Poland, and elsewhere. Some were Orthodox; others were not religious at all. The American West was enriched by the fact that in the centuries-old story of the dispersion of the Jews, people of Sephardic and Ashkenazi heritage found their way into the plains, mountains, and deserts of the region.

Much of the Jewish story in the West is one of shared experience with non-Jews, based on the many needs people have in common. The essential differences were those of belief and issues of conflict born of bias. Perhaps these and other points of view have best been expressed in the words of children. During the latter part of the nineteenth century, a newspaper for Jewish youth, the *Sabbath Visitor*, regularly published letters from across the country in which young authors expressed ideas about their lives. Frequently the themes revealed in letters from the West are those of isolation and despair, a searching for community, or, conversely, a sense of abundance and opportunity.

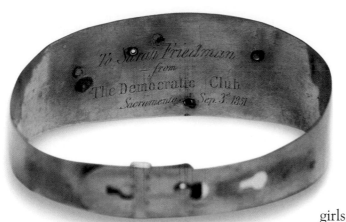

Gold bracelet presented to Sarah Friedman by the Democratic Club of Sacramento, September 3, 1851. Autry Museum of Western Heritage, donated by Ilene Rosengard. Photo by Susan Einstein.

For example, one young man, who signed his letter simply "Cowboy," wrote from Trinidad, Colorado, that "I am all alone in this world, and am an orphan and live out here among the cowboys trying to earn an honest livelihood."[1] Such thoughts of isolation were expressed frequently. Jennie August, from Clay Center, Kansas, lamented that "It is my greatest desire to join with some Jewish boys and girls, because we live in a small town where there is no chance to associate with children of our own religion, although my time passes quickly as I go to school and take music lessons."[2] And young Simon Bitterman of Junction City, Kansas, wrote that "I wish I was as fortunate as some little girls and boys that live in a city where there is a temple, so that I could go to the Sabbath-school and enjoy the Hanuka entertainment ('but if wishes were horses, all beggars might ride'). . . . Mamma showed me a Mezuza to-day, it was the first one I had ever seen."[3]

In many western towns there was not an evident population of Jews. Imagine the scene described by Laura Stenge in Dixon, California, in 1888.

> What do you think happened to me the other day? I will tell you. I went to the Dixon Hall and there were a number of ministers assembled there, and one of them asked me if I love Jesus, and I told him, "No, sir." "And why?" he asked. I told him because I was a Jew. . . . I am very sorry we have no Sabbath-school here, but I enjoy myself in reading your valuable *Visitor*, because it teaches me about our religion.[4]

In sharp contrast, some children living amidst larger, established western Jewish communities expressed enthusiasm for both the locale and its many benefits. Thirteen-year-old Clothilde Cerf, for example, described the Jewish community of Oakland, California, as about "5,000 people and with a Sunday-school of 100 pupils. We have a handsome synagogue, built through the aid of Jews and Gentiles. . . . Our climate is warm, healthy and mild, and our city is constantly growing. We have electric lights and all modern improvements, and also cable cars. We have very good public schools, and I am in the first grade."[5] Across the bay in San Francisco, the Jewish community was even larger and more diverse. George Katz described his hometown as having "a population of 275,000 souls, 20,000 of which are Jewish. There are about ten houses of worship here, one Jewish orphan asylum, four Jewish charitable associations, three cemeteries, and a number of religious schools. I attend the Temple Emanu-El Sabbath-school, and I am very much pleased with the mode of teaching."[6]

One thing is clear from studying the accounts of these Jewish children. From the beginning of the California gold rush to the 1920s, the

Yosemite Valley June 23-8[?]

Shofar (ram's horn) and case. Maker Marcus Jonas, Oakland, California, c. 1870s. Gift of Mrs. Felix Jonas. Courtesy of the HUC Skirball Cultural Center, museum collection. Photo by John Reed Forsman.

West was undergoing the creation of a new order. The immigration of many different peoples is the story of exploiting and developing an entire region, rich with opportunity, fraught with difficulty, and filled with common problems and successes. From Leadville, Colorado, any child could have written about the vibrancy of this community humming in the midst of a great silver strike. But a Jewish youngster wrote that we "have about seventy-five Jewish families here. We have a temple which will comfortably seat about 250 people. We hold Sunday-school every Sunday afternoon. Our little temple cost about $5,000, and was completed a little over two years ago. It was finished and dedicated in just thirty-three days from the day it was commenced."[7]

The American West was arranged and rearranged by many individuals other than cowboys and Indians. A common search for community and opportunity drove many in a similar fashion, and in most cases there were efforts to reestablish or re-create old orders and customs traditional to previous homes and ways of living. Indeed, it is fortunate that the West has always been a land filled with a great variety of environments, resources, and people. There was room for Jewish people along with the hordes of others with differing languages, beliefs, and origins.

Perhaps narrow views of interpreting the region, along with a touch of bias, have helped to obscure the full history of the experience of Jewish life in the American West. One must consider that western Jews were an integral part of most western communities and events. They were evident as participants in the western experience in that they were involved politically, commercially, and socially. Their very presence helps to illustrate that there are many western identities.

The Newmark family (left to right, Carrie Newmark Isaacs, Harris Newmark, Emily Newmark, J. L. Isaacs, Ella Newmark) in Yosemite, 1884. From the Archives of *Western States Jewish History.*

NOTES

1. *Sabbath Visitor* 16, no. 10 (February 1887).

2. *Sabbath Visitor* 16, no. 9 (January 1887).

3. *Sabbath Visitor* 16, no. 10 (February 1887). For similar comments, see also a letter by Annie Alcovich, Carson, Nevada, in *Sabbath Visitor* 16, no. 1 (May 1886).

4. *Sabbath Visitor* 17, no. 12 (April 1888).

5. *Sabbath Visitor* 16, no. 10 (February 1887).

6. *Sabbath Visitor* 14, no. 51 (18 December 1885).

7. *Sabbath Visitor* 17, no. 2 (June 1887).

Looking at America from the West to the East, 1850–1920s

Ava F. Kahn

"THE UNITED STATES IS MY ZION and San Francisco is my Jerusalem," declared Congressman Julius Kahn in 1919.[1] This sentiment reflected the way so many Jews felt about America and about the West. For them, as for the German-born Kahn, the West was no mere home but the promised land that had become inseparable from their treasured Jewish identity.

In American popular culture and scholarship, however, American Jewry has been viewed from the perspective of the legendary New York Jewish immigrant experience. For those Jews who stood on the Pacific shores and settled in western cities and towns, this epic plays only a minor role. For many, their family memories hark back to the diverse communities that have defined the West, not to the distant city of New York.

To this land between the Mississippi River and the Pacific Ocean came a steady stream of Jewish men and women. Between 1850 and the 1920s the Jewish population of the western United States grew from a number too small to count to an estimated 300,000 people.[2] The essays in this book explore the birth of an American Jewish culture that had only tenuous roots in the East. Jewish communities west of the Mississippi blossomed in the mid-nineteenth and early twentieth century in parts of the country that were home to Native Americans before being settled by Spanish conquistadors and missionaries, multiethnic immigrants, and old-stock Americans. Some Jewish men and women built their communities and homes on land with unforgiving high mountains, dry deserts, and

Jewish Hungarian immigrants Adolph and Sam Frankel, pictured here, c. 1920, in Cushing, Oklahoma, entered America through the port of North German Lloyd Wharf in Galveston, Texas, between 1907 and 1914. Photo from Allen Mondell and Cynthia Salzman Mondell's documentary film *West of Hester Street.*

13

Kaspare Cohn's daughter Ray, later Mrs. Ben Meyer. From the Archives of *Western States Jewish History.*

OPPOSITE: Abraham and William Levite, c. 1909. From the Archives of *Western States Jewish History.*

barren plains. If most western Jews were at least tangentially connected to the East, thanks to abundant business and family relationships, the West was their home, and their Jewish community life reflected their western environment. For them, mineral strikes, new railroad routes, crop failures, prairie and downtown fires, and close relations with other Americans were a part of their everyday struggles.

These were important years for Jewish immigration to the United States, with an annual average of 60,488 immigrants reaching America's shores in the latter half of the period.[3] The United States and especially the West offered the incentive of limitless opportunities for advancement no matter one's status at birth. As the American West enticed them, Europe was becoming a more difficult place for Jews to live. Traditional Jewish community life in Europe was disrupted by modernization, which destabilized the political and economic environment. The new economy often did not have a place for small craftsmen, tailors, seamstresses, or merchants, common Jewish occupations.[4] Further disruption in central Europe because of the failed liberal revolutions in 1848 and later the anti-Jewish Russian mob violence of the pogroms of 1881 and 1882, the horrific Kishinev Pogrom of 1903, and the further pogrom in 1905 caused many more Jews to flee a repressive Europe. Others fled to escape military conscription in armies that oppressed Jewish recruits. Moreover, during these years it was becoming especially difficult for Jews to move between cities as restrictive laws were enforced and residency permits were required. Therefore, for many the United States became a land of new beginnings; for some the western United States became the promised land.

By examining the life experiences of Jewish men and women who migrated to the West over land or by sea, who settled in cities and on farms, and who became leaders in the Jewish and larger secular community, the essays in this volume reveal the contrast between the American image of Jews as eastern urbanites and the reality of the diversity of American Jewish life. The authors provide new perspectives on American and western life as well as on the Jewish experience. The pieces are starting points for a discussion of the major regional themes in western Jewish life that carry the story beyond the community and local histories of the last few decades and open the way to a more balanced picture of the West's diverse history.

Surprisingly, American Jewish historians have largely ignored the West except in terms of local or state history. Historians of the West have not to any significant extent even distinguished among the region's diverse European immigrants or related them to one another.[5] As Hasia R. Diner argues in her essay, except for Moses Rischin, American Jewish historians have been fixated on the New York paradigm.[6] Rischin's pioneering anthology, *Jews of the American West*, coedited with John Livingston, features writings that focus especially on local and community history in the Far West.[7] The essays in the present volume build on that work and advance its scholarship thematically. Like the essays authored by Rischin and Earl Pomeroy in *Jews of the American West*, the ones here address larger motifs in western Jewish history, stressing the mobility of the settlers, their step migration to reach the West, their many stops throughout the area, and the effect such travel had on their acculturation. Using the scholarship of *Jews of the American West* as a springboard, the authors of this study give special attention to relations with non-Jews, to the lives of women, to migration patterns, and to the role of Jews in western urban development. Examining regional differences as well as their commonalities, these essays draw comparisons with other sectors, placing the western Jewish experience in a larger American historical context.

The approximately eighty-year period under discussion obviously was critical for the development of the West. Political decisions, transportation revolutions, mineral discoveries, and economic upheavals dramatically affected the day-to-day life of new immigrants and old-time residents alike. Jews migrated for the same reasons as did others—to follow their dreams of adventure, to pursue economic and personal security, and often to search for a healthful climate. After the 1880s, when life became significantly harder in Europe, more and more eastern European Jews

Children at the Denver Sheltering Home for Jewish Children, c. 1912, whose parents were victims of tuberculosis. The home later became the National Home for Asthmatic Children and eventually merged with National Jewish Hospital. Courtesy of the Beck Memorial Archives of Rocky Mountain Jewish History, Center for Judaic Studies and Penrose Library, University of Denver.

immigrated to the United States and the West. For some of them, the open West offered the possibility of becoming farmers and owning land, something that was virtually prohibited for most Jews in eastern Europe.[8] For others, the West offered a new home, where the challenges were often those of founding new secular and religious communities rather than trying to fit into an established order as did their eastern coreligionists.

Taken together, these essays demonstrate the variety in the West's geography and residents as well as the diverse and distinct histories of the Jews who settled there. Many migrants who came to the West were highly mobile, sometimes moving three or four times before finding a place that they could call home. Often they were among the first settlers of a town or region, and they became leaders in both the Jewish community and the community at large. Aside from the Jews who immigrated west directly through the port of Galveston, Texas, many had spent time in the East before venturing west; as a result, they became acculturated and prepared to build western Jewish communities that were a reflection of their new American culture, not simple re-creations of their European lives.[9] Many gained the experience they needed for leadership positions in the West as members of voluntary and fraternal organizations in the East. In the East or in their travels, they unknowingly started the acculturation process, for they worked with people who spoke different languages and practiced a variety of customs. Michael Goldwater, for example, was born in Posen and lived in France and England, where he married the London-born Sarah Nathan, before joining the gold rush.[10] The German-born Henry Cohn peddled throughout the rural East before coming west.[11]

Although many were affected by their stay in the East, that region only partly shaped the newcomers' identity. There were many obvious ties between the Jewish communities of East and West, from business and family relations to the naming in the 1850s of the first two congregations in San Francisco after New York's Emanu-El and Sherith Israel. Throughout the West, from the Korrick's New York store in Phoenix to Philip Schwartz's New York Dry Goods Store in the mining town of Columbia, California, Jewish and non-Jewish clothing merchants alike named their stores after the famous city and so announced that modern, high-quality merchandise was for sale at bargain eastern prices.[12] Except for San Francisco, Jews generally constituted a small percentage of a town's population and were drawn into close relations with their neighbors through business partnerships, fraternal memberships, and civic leadership. As the immigrants and migrants established businesses, started families, and founded Jewish communal life, they became intimately associated with their new hometowns.

There, of course, was no one western Jewish identity. As opposed to the eastern communities, the western Jewish communities were more diverse in their immigrant populations and rapid in their development. The mining rushes attracted migrants not only from the German states but also from France, eastern Europe, England, and the eastern and southern United States. Due to this overwhelming influx of people, the communities formed quickly. For example, the Jewish population of San Francisco, too small to count before 1850, grew to approximately 5,000 by 1860 and to 16,000 by the mid-1870s, while in Denver and the mining districts of Colorado the Jewish population grew from 300 in 1860 to over 10,000 by 1898.[13] In fact, by the 1880s San Francisco, not Chicago or Philadelphia, was the second-largest Jewish community in the United States.[14]

American Jewish History Starting at the Pacific Coast: An Overview

Facing east from the Golden Gate presents a different perspective of western Jewish history than does the view from Castle Garden or Ellis Island. In the mid-nineteenth century, western Jewish communities primarily radiated eastward from San Francisco, not westward from New York, so San Francisco's influence was felt throughout the region. People from the four corners of the world and goods of every description arrived in the port of San Francisco and were conveyed by ship, stagecoach, wagon train, and finally railroad eastward. Merchants formed chains with brothers, cousins, and friends that often helped transport goods from the port towns to the supply towns and onward to the mining and rural towns of the region.

News of the California gold rush brought the first significant Jewish population to the West. In the first five years of the event, close to 6,000 Jews joined the excitement.[15] Most Jewish immigrants caught their first glimpse of San Francisco from a ship's deck, after sailing around Cape Horn or crossing the Isthmus of Panama to board a steamer for the Golden Gate. After journeying from Europe by ship across the Atlantic, most immigrants adjusted to sea travel and chose to avoid the real and perceived far-greater hazards of Indians and illness that threatened wagon trains on a many-month trip on the overland trails.

Once in California, Jews began building community life. Replicating a traditional pattern that was followed throughout the West, San Francisco's Jews established benevolent societies, consecrated burial grounds, and built synagogues. Founding two separate congregations in 1851, the members of Emanu-El and Sherith Israel were initially Orthodox, requiring separate seating for men and women and needing to supply holiday and kosher foods for their members. As they came from different backgrounds, each synagogue followed a different style of religious worship, with Bavarians joining Emanu-El and immigrants from Poland, England, and Russia affiliating with Sherith Israel.[16] Both congregations included Sephardic American-born Jews as members. The two congregations were to pride themselves on their western identities. Indeed, a stained glass window depicting Moses standing in front of El Capitan in Yosemite holding the tablets of the Ten Commandments adorns Sherith Israel's impressive synagogue (see p. 25). Completed just before the 1906 earthquake, it miraculously survived intact, while Emanu-El was devastated. Members of Sherith Israel and Emanu-El alike agreed with their congressman, Julius Kahn, that San Francisco, not New York, was the promised city.

From the outset, the mining economy of the West repeatedly ignited new prosperity. As modern steamships and trains brought migrants and sojourners west, the rapidly growing populations required a wide array of

goods and services. New communities welcomed Jewish merchants, farmers, and tailors as founders and potential civic leaders. In the cities near the Pacific shore and in the mining and farming interior, Jewish life quickly developed, so that by the end of the 1850s the Jewish population in California, Oregon, and Washington had reached 10,000, an impressive number at a time when the total Jewish population of the United States was estimated to be between 125,000 and 200,000.[17] San Diego, Los Angeles, Portland, Seattle, and soon Alaska gave rise to Jewish communities. Most of the founders of these communities had lived in San Francisco or in California's mining towns before heading out for the smaller, developing towns of the West. Many were experienced merchants, seeking out new communities where there was less competition and where their goods and services fueled the town economy and promoted community growth.

Although Jewish occupational, social, and religious life was similar throughout the small-town West, what was different was the physical environment and the diverse populations. When Colorado became a boom mining state with the discovery of gold in the Rocky Mountains in 1859, Jews settled in Denver, Auraria, Leadville, and Central City, just as they had in California, establishing much-needed businesses to supply services to the mining economy. Denver's first synagogue, Congregation Emanuel, was founded in 1874, and the state soon sustained a substantial Jewish community, with several synagogues, significant tubercular hospitals, and an established Jewish social scene. Yet the lives of some of the small Rocky Mountain towns and of their Jewish communities were short, for a mining state's population could not escape the boom-and-bust economy.

In the 1860s, with the U.S. purchase of Alaska from Russia, Jews from San Francisco migrated to the new territory to develop its fur trade. Alaska again attracted Jewish adventurers in the 1890s with the dramatic news of the Klondike gold discovery, and in 1904 a short-lived congregation was established. From the port of San Francisco, Jews also moved eastward to new mining areas in Nevada and Utah. Although Jewish merchants in the Mormon state had to secure the right to establish stores and even to buy and sell property, they did find permanent homes and welcome there, numbering 5,000 by the turn of the twentieth century.[18] In 1916, Simon Bamberger, an immigrant from Germany, was elected Utah's first Democratic and non-Mormon governor. Strongly identified with his new state and with its Jewish community, he served as president of Salt Lake City's congregation B'nai Israel and lobbied both government officials and Jewish philanthropists to encourage Jewish settlement in the state.

Often after sojourns in port cities and mining towns, Jews headed

The Policar family: top, Sol and Ralph Policar; Isaac Policar, his wife, Calo, and their children Sultana, Harry (the first Sephardic child born in Seattle), and Morris, 1911. Courtesy of MSCUA, University of Washington Libraries, neg. no. UW 10432.

Congressman Julius Kahn (c. 1919) served in the U.S. Congress from 1888–1924 (except for 1902–4). Courtesy of the Magnes Museum, Berkeley and San Francisco.

southward to join new communities in Arizona. Even earlier, others had followed trails south to Texas and New Mexico. During and soon after the war with Mexico in the 1840s, the Spiegelberg brothers and other Jewish merchants traveled down the Santa Fe Trail to New Mexico to establish small communities and new mercantile centers. There, Jewish dry goods dealers, bankers, and traders did business and forged relationships with Native Americans, U.S. Army personnel, and migrants and immigrants of all ethnic backgrounds. As was the case throughout the West, chain migrations were common, as the initial settlers were soon followed by brothers, cousins, and other relatives who would soon start their own stores in competition with their predecessors.[19]

Socially isolated from the larger Jewish communities, men often went east or returned to Europe in search of marriage partners, while others married local women, a few becoming prominent in Native American communities. In New Mexico, as it had been earlier in California, the dominant religion when the first Jews arrived was Catholicism, not the Protestantism that dominated most of America. Therefore, to establish civic and social associations, Jews in New Mexico joined Protestant migrants in the minority and sought to forge friendships with the Catholic majority. Although the first bar mitzvah took place in Santa Fe in 1875, before the 1880s there were few religious services other than High Holiday observances.

Merchants' lives throughout the West were changed by the transportation revolution that altered shipping and migration patterns. When the Santa Fe Trail gave way to rail travel, businesses that had boomed on the trail had to adjust to new competition from businesses that located along the railroad tracks. If the 1880s and 1890s saw the birth of several congregations in New Mexico's cities, with the Jewish merchants emerging as community leaders, the total Jewish population remained small, numbering 108 in 1878 and growing only to 858 in 1917.[20]

Although New Mexico did not attract many migrants in the early twentieth century, other western Jewish communities did. The Galveston Movement, led by Jacob Schiff (1847–1920), the distinguished financier

Interior of Korrick's department store, Phoenix, Arizona, 1913. Courtesy of Edgar Korrick and Louise Leibman.

and most-recognized leader of the American Jewish community of the late 1800s and early 1900s, brought immigrants from Europe to the port of Galveston and settled them in communities throughout the West. Between 1907 and 1914, approximately 10,000 Jews entered the United States this way. While some came on their own, most others were prodded west by their eastern brethren. With legislation pending that would restrict immigration, Schiff believed that this plan would mitigate legislators' concerns and reduce the anti-immigrant, anti-Semitic sentiment that was associated with the great numbers of Jewish immigrants who clung to the New York area. Although this plan was paternalist, some new immigrants benefited by being able to settle in less-crowded communities, while others would make their way back to the East, where they had family and friends. Thanks to the Galveston Movement, Jewish communities in Kansas, Texas, Nebraska, Colorado, Iowa, Oklahoma, North Dakota, and California became home to larger numbers of eastern European immigrants.[21]

Millinery store ad from *The Gleaner* (21 October 1864). Courtesy of the Magnes Museum, Berkeley and San Francisco.

Ad for the High Holidays at Beth Yisrael from *The Gleaner* (21 October 1864). Courtesy of the Magnes Museum, Berkeley and San Francisco.

Jewish immigrants who wanted to farm also moved west during the last part of the nineteenth and the early years of the twentieth century. Some believed in communal settlements, others wanted to re-create themselves as farmers, and a small group of experienced farmers and those new to the land became homesteaders. Sponsored by several Jewish organizations and individual benefactors, they founded colonies and family farms in the West reaching from the Dakotas to Oregon and California.[22] While only a few of the homesteaders and colonists succeeded as farmers, the immigrants helped infuse several western Jewish communities with a passion for agriculture that later fed the Zionist movement. In the early twentieth century close to 25,000 Jews resided on farms. Although most lived in New York or New Jersey, many chose to settle west of the Mississippi.[23]

As World War I approached, the children and grandchildren of Jewish immigrants of the middle decades of the nineteenth century be-

came first- and second-generation native-born members of western communities and of a broadly defined American Jewish community. Jews whose forebears had once settled in Germany, Poland, Russia, England, Prussia, Lithuania, and the island of Rhodes now made their homes in San Francisco, Los Angeles, Portland, Seattle, Denver, Dallas, and Omaha. In most cities, Jews who came from different areas had distinct cultures and religious practices; therefore, they often established two or three organizations that served similar functions. For example, in Denver two Jewish-founded tubercular hospitals were established, one by the German community, the other by the eastern European community.[24] By 1913 Seattle had become home to the second-largest Sephardic community in the

Stained-glass window, Congregation Sherith Israel, California Street, San Francisco, showing Moses coming down from Yosemite's El Capitan with tablets on which the Ten Commandments are inscribed. Ben Ailes Photography.

country, surpassed only by New York. These new immigrants even established a Sephardic theater and performed plays in Ladino there.[25] In Los Angeles, Yiddish secularists lived surrounded by palm trees, and Jewish children pretended to be cowboys and cowgirls, while in Oregon, Russian immigrants named their new colony New Odessa after their former home. Although at times these differences caused friction, the sons and daughters of the first immigrants created schools and settlement homes to help later immigrants adjust to western American life. In some western cities where immigrants of diverse heritages and practices lived, religious and secular Jews established schools, hospitals, orphanages, and communal organizations, leading to the mixing of German-Jewish, Sephardic, and Yiddish traditions with western culture.

Beginning in the 1920s and for at least thirty years thereafter, most new settlers in western cities would be migrants, not immigrants coming directly from Europe, as new immigration laws drastically cut Jewish immi-

Newmark Block, junction of
Main and Spring Streets, Los
Angeles, late nineteenth cen-
tury. From the Archives of
Western States Jewish History.

gration from Europe. In 1921 more than 100,000 Jewish emigrants left
Europe for the United States. Three years later, following the passage of
the 1924 Immigration Restriction Act, only 10,000 reached New York.[26]
The years of isolation from Europe that followed would lead to an even
stronger Jewish identification with the West.

The Essays

The following four essays offer new perspectives on Jewish life in the
American West from the mid-nineteenth-century California gold rush to
the closing of the gates of immigration in the early twentieth century.
Chosen for their emphasis on themes of western Jewish life, the pieces
introduce the vast and complex story of Jews in the West. They address
new topics as well as ones that need reexamination. The image of the
Jewish merchant has become a stereotype, yet how western life affected his
status and how in turn he changed the civil leadership in western towns needs

Some of the first Jewish immigrants to enter Galveston Texas, 1 July 1907, under the auspices of the Jewish Immigration Information Bureau. Rabbi Henry Cohen is second from left. Courtesy of the UT Institute of Texas Cultures at San Antonio, no. 73-938.

discussion. Moreover, often left out of explorations of western Jewish life are women and agriculturalists. They too have played roles in creating western Jewish communities, and their voices ring clear in the following writings.

Hasia R. Diner begins our discussion by examining how scholarship and popular culture have presented stereotypes of Jewish life in the East and West. Her thoughtful essay, "American West, New York Jewish," argues that the West often has become the symbol of non-Jewish America, while New York, where so many Jews have lived, has come to symbolize Jewish America. In the West, according to Diner, Jews found a transformative power that made them less Jewish and more truly American.

The subsequent essays analyze what life was really like in the West. Focusing on the experiences of European immigrants, from their arrival on American shores to their integration into western Jewish community life, the pieces examine the common threads of the first seventy-five years of western Jewish life. Jewish westerners were extremely mobile; few outside of San Francisco found permanent homes as soon as they set foot on western soil. Most followed a pattern of step migrations, first settling in the East before coming west. Many traveled far and wide throughout the country until they found a place that they and their children could call home.

"To Journey West: Jewish Women and Their Pioneer Stories" views the American West through the eyes of four Jewish women who settled there between 1850 and 1924. Traditionally the study of westward migration has focused mainly on men. Only recently have the lives of women been receiving serious attention. In the open West, I argue, the lives of Jewish women were notably different from those women who settled in crowded eastern cities. In focusing on the personal experiences of four women, the essay portrays the diversity of Jewish women's lives in the West, discusses regional differences, and examines their relations with non-Jews.

William Toll in his essay explores the role of Jewish merchants in the new towns of the West. From San Francisco and Los Angeles to Trinidad,

The Yiddishe Cowboys & Girls

Roth family gathering in Arizona. From the Roth Collection, Los Angeles.

Colorado; Albany, Oregon; and Prescott, Arizona; Jewish men established Main Street stores supplying virtually all of their customers' needs. Toll discusses not only how these businesses functioned but also emphasizes the merchants' role in affecting migration patterns, family relationships, and religious practices. He argues that the new communities of the West empowered Jewish merchants with the opportunity to transform their lives within one generation.

Finally, in "From Cooperative Farming to Urban Leadership," Ellen Eisenberg examines the lives of Jewish immigrants who arrived in the West at the end of the nineteenth century. In her essay she follows the story of Joseph Nudelman and his family as they travel from Russia across the West from one agricultural colony to another. In this first study of colony life from the immigrant's point of view, Eisenberg uses family documents to present a close look at Jewish life in the Dakotas, Oregon, Nevada, and California. In arguing that the presence of the colonists added significantly to western urban life, even though the colonies failed, Eisenberg has redefined how Jewish leadership emerged in western cities where colonists eventually settled.

Arizona is labeled as "Jerusalem" in another Roth family photo. From the Roth Collection, Los Angeles.

These essays provide an introduction to the diverse region of the western United States and to the multifaceted Jewish communities that developed there. For readers interested in furthering their knowledge of western Jewish life, a selected readings section at the end of this book lists community histories and focused studies. Looking at smaller areas and topics, these sources cover specific communities in greater detail than can be accomplished in regional studies. By covering the entire West and highlighting sectional differences as well as commonalities, these essays are intended to stimulate future research, thought, and discussion of regional themes and to encourage new ways of looking at American Jewish history in the West during the critical first seventy-five years of the great region's history. Many Jewish men and women would come to agree with Congressman Julius Kahn that they had truly reached their promised land.

As editor of this volume, I am very proud to have my name associated with the distinguished work of Hasia R. Diner, William Toll, and Ellen Eisenberg. Their works are a continuation of the studies by Moses Rischin, the quintessential bicoastal American Jewish historian.

THE FAMOUS JOSEPH DRAMA

WITH HIS ELEVEN BROTHERS

Played by Forty-five People

In Eleven Acts

Will Be Presented by the

> **SEPHARDIC CONGREGATIONS OF SEATTLE**
> For the Establishment of a
> Community Fund

SUNDAY, JULY 16, 1922, AT 7 P. M.

At the Washington Hall

14th Ave. and E. Fir St.

TICKETS NOW ON SALE BY THE COMMITTEE

אַנוּנסייֹן

דראמה די אגונסייאֹר אל אינֹורֿאדו פובליקֿו ספֿרדי די סיאֹטלי איל בֿינֿיטֿיינֹטו די לֹה
אימפֿוֹרﬗאטﬗאנֹטי טראֿז/דֿיאה דראֿמאטיקֿה

יוֹסף הצדיק

דראמה אין **11** אקֹטוֹם, ריפֿרֿיוזינטֿאדֿה פֿוֹר **45** אמאטֿוֹריֹם

THE JEWISH VOICE

Playbill of show by the
Sephardic Congregations of
Seattle, 16 July 1922. Courtesy
of MSCUA, University of
Washington Libraries, neg. no.
UW 1023.

NOTES

1. Julius Kahn, *Emanu-El*, 14 February 1919, 11.

2. Jacob Rader Marcus, *To Count a People: American Jewish Population Data, 1585–1984* (Lanham, Md.: University Press of America, 1990). This figure is my addition of the population data from the western states.

3. Jonathan D. Sarna, *The American Jewish Experience* (New York: Holmes and Meier, 1997), 360.

4. Hasia R. Diner, *A Time for Gathering: The Second Migration, 1820–1880*, vol. 2 of *The Jewish People in America* (Baltimore: Johns Hopkins University Press, 1992), 47.

5. For examples of local histories, see the selected readings section. An exception is Frederick Luebke, ed., *European Immigrants in the American West: Community Histories* (Albuquerque: University of New Mexico Press, 1998).

6. See Moses Rischin, ed., *The Jews of the West: The Metropolitan Years* (Berkeley: Western Jewish History Center of the Judah L. Magnes Memorial Museum, 1979).

7. Moses Rischin and John Livingston, eds., *Jews of the American West* (Detroit: Wayne State University Press, 1991), 35.

8. See the Eisenberg essay in this volume.

9. See Ellen Eisenberg, "Transplanted to the Rose City: The Creation of Eastern European Jewish Communities in Portland," *Journal of American Ethnic History* (spring 2000).

10. William M. Kramer and Norton B. Stern, "Early California Associations of Michel Goldwater and His Family," *Western States Jewish Historical Quarterly* 4, no. 4 (1972): 174.

11. Ava F. Kahn, *Jewish Voices of the California Gold Rush: A Documentary History, 1849–1880* (Detroit: Wayne State University Press, 2002).

12. Jerry R. N. Brisco, "The Department Store Industry in Phoenix, 1895–1940" (Ph. D. diss., Arizona State University, 2000).

13. Marcus, *To Count a People*, 28, 33–34.

14. Rischin and Livingston, *Jews of the American West*, 35.

15. Marcus, *To Count a People*, 20.

16. Both congregations later joined the Reform movement.

17. Marcus, *To Count a People*, 181; Sarna, *The American Jewish Experience*, 359.

18. Marcus, *To Count a People*, 218.

19. Earlier, during the Spanish and Mexican periods, Spanish Jews who hid their faith may have lived in the region. However, due to the Inquisition, there is little documentation for their lives as Jews.

20. Marcus, *To Count a People*, 137.

21. For more information about the Galveston Movement, see Bernard Marinbach, *Galveston: Ellis Island of the West* (Albany: State University of New York Press, 1983).

22. For more information about Jewish agricultural settlements, see Selected Readings, pp. 138–39.

23. Robert Alan Goldberg, *Back to the Soil: The Jewish Farmers of Clarion, Utah, and Their World* (Salt Lake City: University of Utah Press, 1986), 42.

24. Jeanne Abrams, "Chasing the Cure in Colorado: The Jewish Consumptives' Relief Society," in Rischin and Livingston, eds., *Jews of the American West*.

25. Marc D. Angel, "History of Seattle's Sephardic Community," *Western States Jewish Historical Quarterly* (October 1974): 22–30.

26. Arthur Goren, *The American Jews* (Cambridge: Harvard University Press, 1982), 73.

American West, New York Jewish

Hasia R. Diner

SINCE THE MIDDLE of the twentieth century, American Jews, particularly as embodied in popular culture and scholarship, have posited a place referred to as "the West" as the essence of America. Their use of this image contrasts boldly with their understanding of New York as the essence of what it means to be Jewish in America. By building this juxtaposition in Jewish geography in their books, films, and other texts of American Jewish culture, they have, in fact, conformed to a dominant mode in American rhetoric, one that views the transformative power of the western frontier as that which has long been essentially American, and the cities, New York in particular, as not quite America.

A notable example of this played itself out in executive producer Steven Spielberg's 1986 cartoon film *An American Tail*. Little Fievel Mousekewitz, his head full of tales of the United States as a place where there were no cats and where the streets were paved with cheese, announced proudly that he was on his way to America. A wiser, older mouse sitting with him in steerage in an immigrant ship corrected him. No, he opined to the little mouse. They were going to New York, and New York was not America.

The Spielberg film illustrated some of the basic metaphors of American Jewish immigration history. Fleeing the pogroms and fooled by stories of boundless wealth, the Mousekewitz family endured a horrific passage across the ocean. They became separated from their youngest offspring,

The Lower East Side, 1880s. From American Jewish Historical Society, Waltham, Massachusetts, and New York, New York.

33

Map of the United States in Yiddish from *Guide to the United States for the Jewish Immigrant,* by John Carr, published under the auspices of the Connecticut Daughters of the American Revolution, 1912. Courtesy of the National Museum of American Jewish History, Maxwell Whiteman Collection, Philadelphia.

די סטייטס, די הױפט שטעט,
טײכען, אָזערעס, ים׳ען און בערג,
אַז די יוניטעד סטײטס.

Los Angeles, North Main Street from Temple Block, c. 1880s. From the Archives of *Western States Jewish History.*

Fievel, who had to make his way in the new land on his own. Once in New York, he encountered greed, exploitation, corruption, and poverty as he searched for his family. The stories he had believed were exposed as a fabrication. There were indeed cats in America.

Not surprisingly for its genre, *An American Tail* ended on an upbeat note. The Mousekewitz family was reunited, and in the process, they, along with their fellow immigrants, organized themselves to combat the evils around them. The optimistic ending of *An American Tail* segued logically into the 1991 sequel, appropriately subtitled *Fievel Goes West.* Fievel, the adventurous and independent one in his family, decided to cast his lot with the real America and head out beyond New York.

Spielberg's use of the theme, cast in comic terms, of the West as the essence of the American experience, deviates from the experience of most American Jews, as reflected in several preceding films, all of which played on the humor of the idea of Jews in the West. Mel Brooks and

36

Andy Bergman's hilarious 1974 comedy *Blazing Saddles* put Yiddish words in the mouths of Indians, while *The Frisco Kid* of 1979, starring Gene Wilder, told the funny story of a Polish rabbi, Avram Belinski, who tangled with Indians and outlaws and brought a Jewish sensibility to the rough and tumble of the "Old West." In 1930 Eddie Cantor's *Whoopee!* involved the incongruous story of a weak, cowardly Jewish businessman who transformed himself in the West, but did so by using his intellect rather than his nonexistent physical prowess.

Cantor's rollicking story of race and role reversals could claim an even earlier popular cultural antecedent, testimony to the long-standing notion that the term *western Jew* was an oxymoron. In 1910 and 1911 two separate silent films appeared with the same title, *Der Yiddisher Cowboy*. In the latter one, Ikey Rosenthal, a down-at-the-heels peddler, took a job at the Bar-X Ranch in Wyoming. Clad in chaps, spurs, and a Stetson hat, Ikey never fit into cowboy culture. With his inherent cleverness, however, his "yiddishe kopp," he outwitted the other cowboys and gained their respect.[1]

Even a serious piece of fiction like Isaac Raboy's *Der Yidisher Kauboy*, which focused on human cruelty amidst the inspiring landscape of the western prairies, pivoted on the incongruity of a Jew in the West.[2] Isaac, the protagonist of Raboy's novel, just like Avram Belinski, Ikey Rosenthal, and even Fievel Mousekewitz, found courage and manliness in the American West. While this novel, unlike the films, was dark and brooding, it involved the same theme of the Jew as the out-of-place westerner. The movies and the Yiddish novel asserted that because Jews, particularly immigrants from eastern Europe, did not belong in the West, the region served for the few as the crucible for turning them into Americans.

The films all pivoted on a joke about Jews, specifically those from Russia and Poland, as ending up somehow in a place where they did not belong. In all of them, a Jewish man, a fresh arrival from the Pale or some such eastern European setting, found himself in an environment to which he was ill-suited. His Jewishness, Yiddish language, and essential weakness set him apart from the "real" westerners. But in his confrontation with the abnormal, he drew upon his Jewish skills, and in the process became something new—an American.

The main currents of American Jewish culture in the twentieth century have posited the big city as the Jews' natural habitat and New York in particular as the city that most suited the Jewish temperament. It was in such an environment that Jews could really be Jewish. Conversely, in the West, the dominant thinking assumed, amidst the cowboys and Indians, on stagecoaches, wagon trains, and horseback, in the small boomtowns and in

Fillmore Street between Post and Sutter Streets, San Francisco, 1909.

"My mother and father saved a little money, they got a store on Fillmore Street, and they had a grocery and delicatessen store. . . . The minute darkness came on, the lights [overarching the street] came on. It was the most beautiful sight, just a beautiful sight." Raye S. Rich, oral history, September 2000.

Courtesy of San Francisco Jews of Eastern European Origins Collection, Western Jewish History Center, Magnes Museum, Berkeley and San Francisco.

the forests, Jews experienced the real America. Here they became less Jewish as they transformed themselves into Americans. The characteristics associated with the West—independence, a disdain for authority, the possibility of starting over, physical courage—have been those traits that Americans have historically imagined to be elements of the American national character.

In a curious irony, in films like *The Frisco Kid* and *Fievel Goes West*, Jewish creators of popular culture texts asserted not only their stake in an American ideology about the transformative and positive power of the West but also the uniqueness of the Jewish people. By admitting that the West represented the best of America and that Jews were anomalies in it, they underscored the ways in which Jews stood out as different from the rest of America. By positing with wonder that any Jews ever lived in the West and repeating the general assumption that Jews were more committed to cities in general and New York in particular, American Jews could proclaim their

Americanness and yet announce the distinctiveness of Jewish culture.

The overarching themes of the films hinged on the serious juxtaposition of the West as America and New York as not quite America. By opting for New York in the main, they, like so many other American Jewish culture texts, asserted that Jews were opting for Jewishness over America. Additionally, the ways in which American Jewish texts have depicted the western experience have served to heighten the stark, but in fact only imagined, difference between Jews from eastern Europe and Jews who had come to the United States earlier in the nineteenth century from Germany and elsewhere in Central Europe.

The New York story, as embedded in American Jewish history, has been that of eastern Europeans, while the story of the Jews in the West has been peopled with "German" Jews. According to the basic narrative, German Jews seemed to be more adaptable and more suited to the West, where they easily fit in. Eastern European Jews were more naturally at home in New York, where they could create and enjoy an authentic Jewish culture.

The information-rich *Pioneer Jews: A New Life in the Far West*, by Harriet and Fred Rochlin, participated in this uninterrogated paradigm about American Jewish history, one which has asserted a fundamental difference between the two "waves" of Jewish immigrants. In all their coverage of the Central European Jewish immigration to the West, the authors used words like *pioneer*, *adventurer*, and most importantly, as they entitled one entire chapter, "Enterprising People." They described the young Jewish men (and to a lesser degree women, since men migrated first and only later found wives) who arrived in western communities before the 1880s as individuals who made rational economic decisions about where best to make a living, establish families, and build lives and communities for themselves. These newcomers quickly integrated into the mainstream and did not segregate themselves. The eastern Europeans, however, were "dressed in bedraggled Old World attire" when they showed up in the West. They made their way there through the assistance of better-off American Jews, unlike those who came before them. Rochlin and Rochlin repeated a common theme, indeed a stereotype, in writing about the post-1880 immigrants from eastern Europe who came to the West: "Too poor, insular, or pious to dwell among the general population, many immigrants gathered together in Jewish quarters, miniatures of New York's Lower East Side . . . [but] in the mild and sunny Far West."[3]

The Rochlin picture book was a piece of popular history. Gerald Sorin's contribution to the American Jewish Historical Society's five-volume *The Jewish People in America* was a piece of fine historical scholarship. How did he treat the "New York versus everywhere else" view of American Jewish history however? First, he separated "New York as the Promised City" from "Beyond New York." Thus, in one chapter, in the book that covered the momentous years from the 1880s through the 1920s, all of America other than New York was studied together as a kind of collective exception to the rule. Sorin admitted that "Jewish life in every city was not identical" but went on to hold up the Lower East Side as the standard against which all other eastern European Jewish enclaves ought to be measured. In discussing the West, and indeed every place outside of New York, Chicago, Boston, and Philadelphia, Sorin saw parallels between the behavior of the earlier German Jewish immigrants and the eastern Europeans who came later. He did not, however, posit that same similarity in the big cities of the East, in particular New York, where he described the new immigrants of the latter part of the nineteenth century as authentic and autonomous creators of a vibrant Jewish culture.[4]

The whole corpus of American Jewish writing about the West assumed a deep comparison between it, regardless of the size of the community, and New York. Writing in 1997 about efforts to restore Los Angeles's Breed Street shul, Jewish newspapers across America claimed that throughout its history the Boyle Heights neighborhood "was dubbed the Lower East Side of Los Angeles." This news item, distributed by the Jewish Telegraphic Agency and carried by numerous Jewish papers, had no evidence to back up the assertion that the throngs of Jews who had lived in Boyle Heights ever considered themselves to be living in a New York enclave on the shores of the Pacific. Rather the story merely assumed that the New York/Lower East Side marker had informed Jewish consciousness seven decades earlier.[5]

Wonder in fact best describes the ways in which American Jewish historians and writers have reacted to and engaged with the fact that Jews lived since the middle of the nineteenth century in Arizona, New Mexico, Oregon, and Montana. They have expressed amazement that Jews were present in Utah and Colorado, the California gold fields, and the Nevada silver mines. That Jews in these places behaved in ways not all that different from Jews in the large cities of the East Coast compounds the sense of amusement and awe that pervades these renditions of the past, both popular and scholarly.

The popular culture representation of the Jewish narrative, particularly as it focused on the experience of eastern European immigrants, reflected the basic outlines of American Jewish culture and conformed to the fundamental narrative of that experience. American Jewish history has been a history of New York. In that narrative, whether told by those who believed that it was between the Hudson and East Rivers where the real American Jewish community existed or if told by those who have maintained that Jews could and should live elsewhere, New York was the theme and everyplace else the variation. In that standard rendition of the American Jewish past, whether New York was criticized and the West lauded, or the reverse, New York has functioned as the epicenter of an imagined Jewish past in a way that was unique.

The histories and popular representations of no other immigrant or ethnic group in America have been so thoroughly dominated by the image of a single city than the New York-centered texts of American Jewry. The Irish, in their writings, have understood that Boston; Chicago; San Francisco; Butte, Montana; and the dozens of mill towns around the Northeast—Pawtucket, Rhode Island; and Lowell, Lawrence, and Waltham, Massachusetts—were as much crucibles for the forging of Irish American culture as was New York, and that no one city dominated the ideology and politics of the others. The descendants of Italian immigrants to the United States have described how San Francisco and Philadelphia, as well as Cleveland, Omaha, and the state of Washington, became home to Italian enclaves; no single Little Italy served as the point of reference for the others. They have, in their historical writings, linked the urban Italian American neighborhoods with a vast network of Italian-owned truck farms that ringed the cities. In that corpus of writing about city and farm, East and West have not been described as opposites; rather, historians have depicted a symbiotic relationship between the smaller and larger communities. Likewise, the Chinese in America have developed a historical consciousness based upon a bicoastal perspective, with New York and San Francisco each credited with housing a thriving and vibrant community.

In the histories of African American communities, large and small, East Coast and West Coast, in the Midwest and New England, scholars have focused on a single story told about different places. Regardless of the size of the city—Boston or Evansville, Indiana; New York or Milwaukee—black Americans have endured but resisted oppression, built communities, and created cultural institutions that served their needs. The reason why scholars of black communities have embarked on studying any particular community has not been to show how big a community was, how influential it was, or how it dominated other, smaller communities. Rather, large communities and tiny ones all demonstrated the singular history of oppression and resistance, played out in many different localities.

American Jewish histories, by contrast, have basically measured how much a community resembled New York or how much impact New York had upon it. As analyzed by historians and as depicted in popular culture narratives, only Jews have used a single city to represent the entire experience of their past in America. American Jewish culture since the end of the nineteenth century and American Jewish history as a scholarly enterprise of the latter part of the twentieth century have obsessed on New York as the norm, and everywhere else in America where Jews lived has been viewed as an exception. Both the collective memory and the historical writings consider American Jewry from the perspective of New York, and both react in a kind of astonishment at the knowledge that Jews lived elsewhere and went to considerable efforts to live Jewish lives while also coming to terms with American demands and opportunities.

Nothing in the retrospective literature might best exemplify this tendency to universalize from New York than the writings of Irving Howe, the literary critic who wrote *The World of Our Fathers*, probably the best-known, most widely disseminated and discussed text in American Jewish culture. Howe understood American Jewry as being synonymous with New York and the history of eastern European Jewish immigration to be one and the same with the life of the Lower East Side. He boldly subtitled his magnum opus *The Journey of the East European Jews to America and the Life They Found and Made There*. With the exception of a brief description of the Am Olam movement, the utopian band of Russian Jewish émigrés who settled in New Odessa, Oregon, in the early 1880s, Howe had virtually nothing to offer about the migration and settlement of Jews from eastern Europe to America west of New York.[6]

Following upon the success of *The World of Our Fathers*, Howe, in collaboration with Kenneth Libo, put together two picture books, loosely connected by essays. In the first book, *How We Lived: A Documentary History of Immigrant Jews in America, 1880–1930*, Howe and Libo amassed a visually pleasing array of photographs of people and places and reproductions of posters, newspaper headlines, and advertisements. *How We Lived*, like *The World of Our Fathers*, took America to mean New York. It included no words, pictures, or images of any place west of the Hudson. It also illustrated few spaces in New York outside the Lower East Side. New York and its Lower East Side functioned here as the heart and soul of Jewish America. Catalogers at the Library of Congress, it seems, were not fooled by Howe and Libo's title. They understood that despite the word *America* in the title, *How We Lived* was a book about New York, so they gave it a call number under New York history.[7]

Five years later Howe and Libo decided to treat the rest of America

Playbill from the 1922–26 Jewish Theatrical Company, organized by the Josephson family at the Palm Theatre on West Colfax in Denver. Courtesy of the Beck Memorial Archives of Rocky Mountain Jewish History, Center for Judaic Studies and Penrose Library, University of Denver.

left out of *How We Lived*. In 1984 they informed their readers, expressed with a degree of astonishment, that some Jews could have said "we lived there, too," publishing *We Lived There, Too: In Their Own Words and Pictures Pioneer Jews and the Westward Movement of America, 1630–1930*.[8] Every place west of New York found its way into the category "too."

This mode of describing Jewish residence and community west of New York has continued to function as the dominant paradigm in the quarter century since *The World of Our Fathers*. As previously mentioned, Gerald Sorin characterized Jewish life outside of the "Promised City" as "Beyond New York." Even in an essay charging American Jewish historians to write about the West and to take seriously the authoring of local community accounts, the historian Marc Lee Raphael told them to go—again—"Beyond New York."[9]

In a similar vein, historians writing about western Jewish communities have, since the 1960s, felt called upon to compare and contrast their subject with New York. Steven Lowenstein, for example, authored an excellent and thorough history of the Jews of Portland, Oregon. He argued convincingly that Jews ought to know the history of the communities in which they lived and that "it is not only in Israel, in Europe, in the East or Midwest, but in Oregon—this beautiful outpost of the Diaspora—where we have chosen to live our lives." But when Lowenstein began to describe the arrival of eastern European Jews in Portland at the end of the nineteenth century, he included a photograph of New York's Hester Street, bearing the caption: "Hester Street was a ferment of activity. Most immigrants to Oregon who came from eastern Europe spent their first weeks in America on New York's Lower East Side." Lowenstein offered no evidence for this assertion nor did his statement add anything to the history of Portland Jewry.[10] Likewise, a recent historical portrait of Denver Jewry during the era of the eastern European Jewish migration asserted that, with the arrival of the newcomers, Denver "soon resembled the Lower East Side of New York with its many synagogues, small businesses, and adherence to an Orthodox Jewish tradition."[11]

Historians and others who have written about the American Jewish past have relied on the theme of New York versus everywhere else in part because of the realities of numbers. Certainly, New York was the behemoth of Jewish communities in America. In 1907, 33 percent of American Jews, or 600,000 people, lived there. By 1927, its share had climbed to 44 percent, or 1,765,000 people. New York's closest rival was Chicago, which in those two years housed 5.6 percent (100,000 individuals) and 8 percent (325,000 individuals) of the Jews in the United States. Los Angeles, the western city that came closest to New York, had 7,000 Jewish residents in 1907 and 65,000 in 1927. Trailing behind was San Francisco, which in 1880 had been second only to New York in its Jewish population. As other places grew, however, its Jewish population did not keep up. Although in 1907 its Jewish population of 30,000 was larger than that of Los Angeles, this number barely grew in the subsequent two decades. In 1927 it was frozen at 35,000. Denver had 5,000 Jews in 1907 and 17,000 twenty years later.[12]

Not only did more Jews live in New York than in any other place, in no other location did Jews constitute so large a percentage of the local population. While in Philadelphia, itself a massive Jewish population center, Jews constituted 11 percent of the city's residents, in New York in 1920 they accounted for over a quarter of the city.[13] New York in general and the Lower East Side in particular pulsated with Jewish life, as did neighborhoods like Brownsville and Williamsburg in Brooklyn as well as Harlem and Washington Heights in upper Manhattan. Signs on stores, periodicals hawked from newsstands, and the sounds of buyers and sellers of distinctively Jewish goods and services all demonstrated the intensity of New York's Jewish presence.[14]

The fact that the Yiddish press and theater emanated from New York also explains the New York focus of both scholarship and popular thinking. These two powerful cultural institutions, which disseminated Jewish culture to Jews far beyond the Hudson, meant that New York established itself as the production center of American Jewish culture. The Yiddish newspapers of New York, like *Forverts*, published local editions for other cities, in the process establishing New York as the Jewish center. Theatrical companies from New York as well as solo Yiddish performers like Molly Picon spent the summer months touring, bringing theatrical offerings to

Yiddish audiences across the continent.[15] Writing about Chicago, hardly a remote frontier outpost, for example, the sociologist Louis Wirth noted in 1927: "The Chicago Yiddish theater, like the Yiddish press, is for the most part but a sideshow of the New York ghetto. The Yiddish newspapers and the Yiddish theater draw their talent from New York. And if there happens to be discovered a literary genius or an *actorke* in the local scene, the wider and more appreciative audience of Second Avenue—the Yiddish Broadway of New York—soon snatches them off."[16]

Looking back on the history of American Jewry, writers have also understood the West to be anomalous because so many of the activities of American Jewish organizations and their leaders in the late nineteenth and early twentieth centuries defined New York as a problem. Middle-class American Jews, usually American born, not only bought into the American ideology, as reflected in Frederick Jackson Turner's "frontier thesis" of the West as the great safety valve that defused the social unrest of the cities, but they believed that if Jews dispersed to smaller, western communities, anti-Semitism would decline.

Between 1901 and 1922, for example, the Industrial Removal Office (I.R.O.), a charitable society backed in large measure by the Baron de Hirsch Fund and the financier Jacob Schiff, sent about 75,000 eastern European Jewish immigrants out of New York and off to the West. The men who applied to participate in the program ended up in about fifteen hundred places outside of New York. Here, the project's supporters hoped, they would find work, adapt to America, and avoid the pitfalls of life in America's largest city. The I.R.O. scheme was based on the idea that when too many Jews crowded together in one place—namely New York—they suffered from the harsh realities of the urban industrial economy and drew the attention of non-Jews. In the latter case, Jewish urban concentration fed into the worst fears of anti-Semites, who exploited the immigrant Jews' economic plight for their own nefarious ends. Leo N. Levi, a B'nai B'rith official from Texas, exclaimed that the I.R.O. could save Jews from "a worse hell than was ever invented by the imagination of the most vindictive Jew-hater of Europe." Understood by both givers and takers as an opportunity to move some Jews from east to west, the I.R.O. stands in American Jewish history as an example of the complex mix of philanthropy, benevolence, antiurbanism, fear of anti-Semitism, and condescension that emanated from the "top down," coloring relations between eastern European immigrant Jews and the Jews already present in America.[17]

The 1907 "Galveston Plan," instituted by the Jewish Immigrants Information Bureau and totally funded by Jacob Schiff, also sought to divert eastern European Jewish immigrants away from New York and to remake Jewish life in America in a western image. Since Galveston itself offered few prospects for making a living, Schiff, Rabbi Henry Cohen, and Morris Waldman, all involved in the enterprise, assumed that the Jews who entered the United States through the Texas port would fan out through the American heartland, avoid the crowding problem of the big cities, and in the process be less obvious or obtrusive as Jews.[18]

The scope of these projects to facilitate the migration of Jews out of New York and into the supposedly more benevolent climate of the West reflects the skewed geographic perspective of American Jewry. It understood New York to be the problem that most afflicted the immigrant newcomers and considered any place outside of New York as somehow the West. In order to thin the ranks of New York Jewry, the I.R.O. sent Jewish immigrant men not only to Cedar Rapids, Iowa; El Paso, Texas; Oklahoma City; and a variety of other small western towns but also to St. Louis, Cleveland, and Chicago.

These latter cities did not carry the cultural baggage of New York. Despite the poverty, poor working conditions, and crowding endured by immigrant Jews in these places, there was not the same sense of fear that Jews in New York experienced. The actions of the I.R.O., however, made sense in the context of an emerging Jewish culture in America that defined New York as the core and everything else, regardless of where it was, as the periphery. It also made sense in an American culture that increasingly equated the terms *New York* and *Jewish*, while any place in the periphery stood for America.

That Jews from New York (and elsewhere in the East) came to Denver to be cured of tuberculosis helped confirm the view of the transformative impact of the West. They flocked to Denver, like many other consumptives, because of the city's dry, clean climate. Most of the health-seekers, Jew and non-Jew alike, were poor, and Denver Jews, led by Frances Wisebart Jacobs, campaigned and organized to rationalize and improve the city's medical facilities. In 1899 the B'nai B'rith opened the National Jewish Hospital for Consumptives in Denver to serve New York's ailing Jews, known commonly as "lungers." To solidify the image of Denver—and the West—as the best hope for sick Jews, Dr. Charles Spivak helped to found in 1904 the Jewish Consumptives Relief Society, also based in Denver. Although the two tuberculosis hospitals competed with one another, they managed to collaborate in 1908 and jointly create a home for the children of the hospitalized consumptives (see p. 17). The many fund-raising campaigns, the articles in the Jewish press, both in English and

Yiddish, and the wondrous tales told by recovered Jews who returned to the East added to the aura of the West as the place where Jews could be remade and remake themselves.[19]

For many of the philanthropists, rabbis, journalists, and social commentators within the Jewish world, New York epitomized urban life and its attendant woes. They defined New York as a problem to be solved. For most of the hundreds of thousands of Jews who lived there during the immigrant era, social amelioration would come by improving conditions at home. Organizations like the I.R.O. hoped that salvation would come by finding new homes, west of New York's urban squalor.

The problem with the general presentation about Jews in the West and their integration into America on the one hand and their deviance from the American Jewish norm on the other grows out of the actual details of American Jewish history. The conventional analysis overstates the distinction between "German" and "Russian" Jews, a dichotomy that runs through the literature but has little basis in fact. Eastern European Jews showed up in America well before the American Revolution, and the process of their integration into the newly emerging nation was no different than that of Jews from western and central Europe.[20]

Jewish migration in the years from the 1820s through the 1880s, the supposed era of the "German" migration, included Jews from Posen, a Polish province incorporated into Prussia, as well as from parts of Austria-Hungary, Lithuania, and even western Russia.[21] Indeed, the first Jews to show up in such very western places as the California gold fields, territorial Arizona, and early Los Angeles, starting in the 1850s, hailed from eastern Europe. Eastern European Jews who peddled in the West from the middle of the nineteenth century through the early decades of the twentieth century differed not at all from Jews from Central Europe who took their first steps into the American economy through this very route. Timing of the migration rather than European place of origin proved to be a more crucial factor.

American Jews, inside and outside the ranks of professional historians, have persisted in thinking about the Germans as the Americanizers and the eastern Europeans as those committed to an authentic Jewish culture. They have likewise associated the former with the earlier period and the latter with the later era. In addition, the tendency has been to link the German accommodationists with the West and the eastern Europeans, with their commitment to a vibrant Jewish life and culture, with the East.

This therefore gives American Jewish memory its basic New York versus the West dichotomy, which by and large dovetails with a German versus eastern European binary. But when looking at the details of Jewish life in the West, the differences emerge as less stark. Whether in the larger cities, like Los Angeles, Denver, Portland, San Francisco, and Seattle, or in smaller communities, such as Boise, Helena, Fargo, and Trinidad, immigrant Jews, regardless of where they came from, engaged in a process of building their families and constructing Jewish communities. They found ways to institute the basic practices of traditional Jewish life and to create the kinds of institutions—synagogues, cemeteries, schools, *mikvaot* (ritual baths), facilities for providing kosher food—that existed throughout the Jewish world regardless of place. These western Jews, just like East Coast Jews, defined the details of Jewish life important to their lives. Obviously the smaller the community, the harder to provide for the needs of Jewish communal life and ritual practice. But this would include Tupper Lake, New York, or Beaver Falls, Pennsylvania, no less than the Dakota prairie.

When the spirit of Reform swept through Europe and the United States, it whipped through New York as surely as it did Portland, Salt Lake City, and San Francisco. The struggle between traditionalists and reformers informed New York and Denver congregations in a similar manner, and the strategies employed to foster a particular kind of Judaism had more to do with community size than geographic location. As a case in point, in 1915 more-observant Jews in Salt Lake City, despite the relative smallness of the community, seceded from B'nai Israel. Just as Jews were doing in New York, the Utah secessionists formed a more-traditional congregation, Shaarei Tzedek, where they maintained a strict ban on mixed seating.[22]

Throughout the continent, with western communities as no exception, Jews created institutions of Jewish life to suit their needs. The history of the West has largely been told as the history of Reform and adaptation to America, and that of New York has been framed around the details of Jews creating autonomous and vibrant cultural institutions. But in fact Jews in the West behaved no differently than Jews in New York when it came to shaping institutions to fit their Jewish identities. For instance, Orthodox Jews from Congregation Montefiore in the 1920s in Salt Lake City bought a substantial house, which they named Covenant House and devoted to youth activities. Jews in this western city, the Mormon capital of the world, put on Jewish dramas and debates, socialized with each other, and created a distinctively Jewish space.[23]

Although New York Jews have been described throughout the literature as the creators and sustainers of Yiddish culture, San Francisco Jews also established their own Yiddish theatrical groups in the 1890s, albeit on an amateur level,[24] and in the early decades of the twentieth century

Yiddish newspapers were published in San Francisco (*Der Emes*), Portland (*Der Yiddisher Geist*), and elsewhere in the West.[25] In Los Angeles in the 1920s a full-scale Yiddish culture bloomed. The 40,000 Jews who lived there consumed Yiddish plays, lectures, and newspapers. They had their own playwrights, novelists, poets, and actors. They had ideological and aesthetic arguments and did not use New York as the point of reference for Jewish matters.[26] The Yiddish poet Joseph Katzenogy described Los Angeles in 1925 as "intoxicated by the smell of orange blossoms/blinded by the towering mountains/refreshed by the proud palms."[27] Likewise, several thousand women and men showed up on April 2 and 3, 1912, at Seattle's Moore Theater to hear a performance by "the celebrated Yiddish Prima Donna Madam Regina Prager." Her recital of "Hadassah, Froyen Liebe," or "Women Love," was advertised in this very western city as being staged in honor of the upcoming Passover holiday. The poster advertising Madam Prager's concert linked the Jews of Seattle with audiences all over the Jewish world, without New York as the mediator of Jewish culture in America.[28]

In both New York and the West, among eastern European Jews and the earlier immigrants from Central Europe, business of one kind or another represented the Jewish economic metier. Across America some Jews, regardless of where they came from or where they settled, spent some part of their lives in peddling. The larger the city, the more likely the peddling took place on urban streets, while the smaller the community, chances were that peddlers left home during the week to hawk their goods to farm families for some part of their career. Either way, the economic enterprise was the same.

In the latter decades of the nineteenth century and the early years of the twentieth, big-city Jews showed up among the ranks of industrial laborers, in the garment trade in particular, as they had never before. That industry, while centered in New York, also employed Jewish workers in Chicago and Los Angeles. Notably, Jews in the West since the 1850s had been involved in the sewing of clothes, although until the end of the nineteenth century they did so not in large industrial settings but in workshops connected to stores that sold directly to the public. The story of Jacob Davis provides an important case in point. While the name of a Bavarian immigrant, Levi Strauss, has been affixed to a globally recognized product—Levis denim jeans—in one rendition of the history of the garment the true creator of the "gents" work pants was a Russian Jewish tailor living in Reno, Nevada, in the 1870s, one Jacob Davis.[29]

The degree to which New York served as the heart of the American garment industry may have indeed been one of the most notable phenomena that separated it from the rest of America.[30] Yet even here historians have been so focused on the history of the union movement in the garment industry that they have failed to note that eastern European immigrant Jews in New York, just like Jews in the West, opted for small businesses as soon as they could.

By emphasizing the centrality of New York as the essence of the American Jewish experience and the West as the emblem of the Jews' encounter with America, American Jews have attempted to express themselves in both American and distinctively Jewish terms. New York and the West have to be represented as different because the two places serve different ends in American Jewish consciousness. The New York part of the equation functions as the narrative that emphasizes their resistance to assimilation, to the tenacity of *yiddishkeit*, as imported from eastern Europe. The West has functioned as the place from which they emphasize their embrace of America and its transformative power. They have wanted to be both Americans and Jews and have created a regionally bifurcated story that allows one place—New York—to tell one part of their tale and the West to express the other.

NOTES

1. Lester D. Friedman, *The Jewish Image in American Film* (Seacaucus, New Jersey: Citadel Press, 1987), 21.

2. Isaac Raboy, *The Yiddish Cowboy*, ed. Nathaniel Shapiro (Westfield, New Jersey: Tradition, 1989); originally published as *Der Yidisher Kauboy* (New York: Folks Farlag Alveltlekher, 1945).

3. Harriet Rochlin and Fred Rochlin, *Pioneer Jews: A New Life in the Far West* (Boston: Houghton Mifflin, 1984), 216.

4. Gerald Sorin, *A Time for Building: The Third Migration, 1880–1920*, vol. 3 in *The Jewish People in America* (Baltimore: Johns Hopkins University Press, 1992), 136–37.

5. Quoted in Hasia R. Diner, *Lower East Side Memories: The Jewish Place in America* (Princeton: Princeton University Press, 2000), 34.

6. Irving Howe, *The World of Our Fathers: The Journey of the East European Jews to America and the Life They Found and Made There* (New York: Harcourt Brace Jovanovich, 1976), 84–86.

7. Irving Howe and Kenneth Libo, *How We Lived: A Documentary History of Immigrant Jews in America* (New York: St. Martin's Press, 1979).

8. Kenneth Libo and Irving Howe, *We Lived There, Too: In Their Own Words and Pictures Pioneer Jews and the Westward Movement of America, 1630–1930* (New York: St. Martin's/Marek, 1984).

9. Marc Lee Raphael, "Beyond New York," in Moses Rischin and John Livingston, eds., *Jews of the American West* (Detroit: Wayne State University Press, 1991), 52–65.

10. Steven Lowenstein, *The Jews of Oregon, 1850–1950* (Portland: Jewish Historical Society of Portland, 1987), xii, 75–76.

11. *A Colorado Jewish Family Album: 1859–1992* (Denver: Rocky Mountain Jewish Historical Society, 1992), 14.

12. Lee Shai Weissbach, "The Jewish Communities of the United States on the Eve of Mass Migration," *American Jewish History* 78 (September 1988): 79–108.

13. Sorin, *A Time for Building*, 136.

14. Diner, *Lower East Side Memories*.

15. Molly Picon, *So Laugh A Little* (New York: Paperback Library, 1966).

16. Louis Wirth, *The Ghetto* (Chicago: University of Chicago Press, 1928), 225.

17. Robert Rockaway, *Words of the Uprooted: Jewish Immigrants in Early Twentieth-Century America* (Ithaca: Cornell University Press, 1998), 13, 11, 50; Jack Glazier, *Dispersing the Ghetto: The Relocation of Jewish Immigrants across America* (Ithaca: Cornell University Press, 1998).

18. Bernard Marinbach, *Galveston: Ellis Island of the West* (Albany: State University of New York Press, 1983).

19. Alan Kraut, *Silent Travelers: Germs, Genes, and the "Immigrant Menace"* (New York: Basic Books, 1994).

20. Eli Faber, *A Time for Planting: The First Migration, 1654–1820*, vol. 1 of *The Jewish People in America* (Baltimore: Johns Hopkins University Press, 1992).

21. Hasia R. Diner, *A Time for Gathering: The Second Migration, 1820–1880*, vol. 2 of *The Jewish People in America* (Baltimore: Johns Hopkins University Press, 1992).

22. Juanita Brooks, *History of the Jews of Utah and Wyoming* (Salt Lake City: Western Epics, 1973), 173.

23. Ibid.

24. Nahma Sandrow, *Vagabond Stars: A World History of Yiddish Theater* (Syracuse: Syracuse University Press, 1977).

25. See the periodical catalog of the Dorot Jewish Division of the New York Public Library.

26. Max Vorspan and Lloyd P. Gartner, *History of the Jews of Los Angeles* (San Marino, California: Huntington Library, 1978), 141–42.

27. Quoted in Diner, *Lower East Side Memories*, 34.

28. A reproduction of the poster can be found in Rochlin and Rochlin, *Pioneer Jews*, 219.

29. Rochlin and Rochlin, *Pioneer Jews*, 56.

30. Nancy L. Green, *Ready-To-Wear, Ready-To-Work: A Century of Industry and Immigrants in Paris and New York* (Durham: Duke University Press, 1997).

To Journey West: Jewish Women and Their Pioneer Stories

Ava F. Kahn

"**E**ARLY IN FEBRUARY IN 1907 we took the train to the Promised Land." This is how Minnie Landman described her trip to Wyoming.[1] To many Jews the Promised Land remained Israel. For some immigrants, however, this dream shifted to the promised city of New York, while for others the land promised was further west. For Fanny Brooks it was Utah; for Mary Goldsmith Prag, California. Flora Langermann Spiegelberg settled in New Mexico, while Leah Landman built a home on the Wyoming prairie.

Studying the lives of women who traveled west is a relatively new field. In recent years, following the work of Lillian Schlissel and other prominent historians, the field has matured. This interest, combined with the publication of several outstanding works in American Jewish women's history, has led to the issuing or reissuing of memoirs and collected biographies describing the diverse lives of Jewish women in the West.[2] Harriet Lane Levy wrote of her privileged childhood in post–gold rush San Francisco, Sophie Trupin described her life in rural North Dakota, and Linda Mack Schloff wrote an excellent collective biography of Jewish women in the upper Midwest.[3] However, very few western Jewish women left detailed stories for future generations. Some are only known by a few documents or memories. Even though most of these women's lives are not recorded in history books, their identities as westerners helped shape both western life and a new western Jewish community life.

Engagement photo of Flora Langermann (Spiegelberg), age sixteen, 1873. Courtesy of her great-granddaughter Sue R. Warburg, San Francisco.

53

VIEW OF MARYSVILLE.

View of Marysville, California, 1853. Courtesy of the Bancroft Library, University of California, Berkeley.

The stories of Fanny Brooks, Mary Goldsmith Prag, Flora Langermann Spiegelberg, and Leah Landman do not make a uniform statement about existence in the West but rather convey the diversity of experiences there. An examination of their lives reveals that because of the challenges of frequent relocation and frontier surroundings, these women developed the ability to adapt to new places and extreme mobility.

Many Jewish women followed their fathers, brothers, and husbands west, some reluctantly, while a few Jewish women made the decision to travel alone, excited by the prospects of a new life. Once these women had left their native lands, additional wagon, train, or boat trips became commonplace for them. Before coming west, many women lived in the East, where they learned the language and customs of their new land. Many were well on their way to becoming Americans when they journeyed to their new western homes. Having traveled in Europe and the eastern United States, they had learned how to work with non-Jews, a skill that would be beneficial in the less-Jewish West. As economic cycles changed, western women were often uprooted. Likely to be among the first settlers of a town or region, Jewish women were often called upon to be community founders and civic leaders, creating institutions and fighting for causes that affected the general as well as the Jewish community.

The first major pull to the western United States came in the 1850s, during the height of the California gold rush, when Jewish men and women became shopkeepers in cosmopolitan San Francisco and the volatile mining towns. Fanny Brooks, a tall girl with dark hair and eyes, was a new bride of seventeen when she came west. The daughter of a family that could trace its lineage of scholars and merchants back to fifteenth-century Italy and Greece, Fanny left Prussia in 1853 to travel throughout the West, settling first in a small mining town, then San Francisco, and finally in the Mormon capital, Salt Lake City.[4] Knowledge of Fanny's travels and thoughts has been gleaned from letters and an extensive narrative written by her daugh-

Timbuctoo, California, 1850s. Courtesy of the Bancroft Library, University of California, Berkeley.

ter Eveline, which describes events Fanny related to her.

Born in Poland, the young Mary Goldsmith Prag traversed Nicaragua riding in front of her father on a mule, eventually reaching San Francisco by steamship in 1852. Although she grew up in this bustling city, her life would take her to Utah and then back to California to become one of San Francisco's first female Jewish leaders. Mary's life is well documented; as a public figure and author, she left speeches and several memoirs to record her experiences.

Flora Langermann Spiegelberg, born in New York and raised in California and Germany, crossed the country twice as a child. In 1875, as a young bride, she followed the dangerous Santa Fe Trail with her husband to Santa Fe, New Mexico. In that new frontier town she raised a family and became a Jewish community leader. Later, on her return to New York City, she became an author, penning stories of her life in the remote Southwest.

A pioneer of the Wyoming prairie, Leah Landman left Russia for Austria and then England. She crossed the ocean to Pittsburgh before taking the train west to Wyoming in 1907 and learning the life of a farmer's wife on the western plains. Her daughter Minnie, born in Pittsburgh, recorded the family history, paying special attention to her mother's trials and tribulations.

Taken together, these four stories create a new understanding of the lives of Jewish women in the western United States. Jewish women in the West arrived with different abilities and faced challenges that were unlike those faced by their eastern counterparts.

FANNY BROOKS
(1838–1901)
From Breslau to
Utah: A Life
of Travel

Fanny Brooks traveled much of her life. From a wagon pulled by mules to luxury ocean liners, all forms of conveyance brought her to different phases of her existence. Although no life in the West can be said to be typical, Fanny's travels, family experiences, and early hardships were similar to those of many wives who came west. These women, often married to men who were always looking for fresh opportunities for success, started new

homes only to pick up stakes and move on in serial fashion throughout the West. Educated and adventurous, Fanny joined the western rush for the same reasons as many men: she did not want to stay at home in a small Prussian village near Breslau, when the United States offered such excitement. In 1853 her Uncle Julius Gerson Brooks (changed from Bruck) returned home from the eastern United States to the village where his widowed mother ran a small dry goods store, telling fantastic stories of his five years living in a country with wild Indians and money growing on trees. Fanny wanted to return to the United States with him. Like many homesick Jewish immigrants, Julius had returned home to visit his family and possibly find a bride. When his sixteen-year-old niece asked to accompany him on his travels, Julius replied, "The only way that you can come is to marry me." She answered, "If my parents do not object, I will."[5] Julius did not ask for a dowry, and they were soon married.

After the ceremony, they left by the port of Hamburg for a three-week crossing to New York. Unlike many of her peers, Fanny was a graduate of a girls' school.[6] On the ship she socialized with other passengers, speaking German and French and quickly learning English. In addition, she entertained her fellow shipmates by playing the piano and guitar. When they arrived in New York, there was news of the discovery of gold in California. "[B]oys were selling papers calling out gold excitement . . . everyone who could possibly go was selling his property to raise money to go west—so [Julius] said why stay in New York when everyone is going west? [Fanny] agreed."[7] After spending five months in a Jewish boardinghouse in New York preparing for an overland trip, the Brookses set off for California by way of Galena, Illinois. There they waited over a month for news of a wagon train west. This stopover forced Fanny to socialize with immigrants and American-born alike. While staying at an inn, Fanny observed American cooking and customs and heard stories of the frontier West and of Yankee life in New England. These experiences helped prepare her for a new life in the multiethnic West.

Joining a wagon train in Florence, Nebraska, Fanny and Julius journeyed west through the summer and fall. Traveling as one of a hundred wagons, they experienced the hardships of western travel as well as the bonding experiences that come from stressful conditions and forced symbiotic friendships. Eveline's memoir emphasizes humorous stories, while the tragedies of the trip are barely mentioned. For example, the memoir notes in passing that Fanny lost her first child during a cold spell while traveling between Laramie and Sweetwater, but it gives a detailed description of a first try at baking bread. As she had never baked bread before, she

Fanny Brooks, her daughter Eveline, and unknown baby, c. 1861. Courtesy of the Bancroft Library, University of California, Berkeley.

neglected to use yeast and was distraught when her bread did not rise. As Eveline records her mother's story, Fanny's neighbors on the train saw her crying, gave her biscuits for breakfast, and in the evening taught her how to use yeast and make a fine bread. To repay them, Fanny taught the women how to bake a German coffee cake. More than just teaching her a skill she would need in her new western home, this cultural exchange reinforced Fanny's confidence in working with women of all nationalities, an ability she would use her entire life.

Fanny was the master of their two-mule team. Although others tried to drive them, the mules would only go when she was at the reins. Crossing deep and swift rivers and keeping a watch for hostile Indians, Fanny and Julius reached Salt Lake City in the fall of 1854. There they spent the winter, as it was too late in the year to continue their journey to California. In this Mormon city they met a German Jew who had converted to the Mormon faith. He proclaimed Fanny to be the first Jewish woman coming overland to reach that city. This may or may not be true. However, she was probably one of the first to journey overland to California. Most Jews traveled to California by ship. Julius may have chosen the overland route because he had a strong dislike for sea travel.

In the spring of 1855 the Brookses continued west. Julius opened a general merchandise store in the river supply town of Marysville, California, where they made their home for four years. Named for a survivor of the Donner party, Mary Murphy Clovillaud, the wife of the town's principal landowner, it was founded in 1842 near the confluence of the Feather and Yuba Rivers on property that formerly belonged to John Sutter. Because of its proximity to the northern mining region and the heavy river trade, Marysville had a growing Jewish merchant community. Fanny's brother Max Brooks was a member of Marysville's Hebrew Benevolent Society, and the community had an active social life.[8] In October of 1856 seventy couples assembled at the Marysville city hall to hold a dinner dance to benefit the Hebrew Benevolent Society. Describing the event, the local paper was full of praise: "The music was exquisite. . . . Never has there been a Ball in our city, where so much pain was taken, and with so much success, to make each feel that he was a favored guest."[9] This was a fundraising event, for the society needed funds to care for the needy and sick and to bury the indigent dead. It first consecrated a cemetery in 1855.

During her four years in Marysville, Fanny gave birth to three children; the oldest, Amelia, died in Marysville at the age of one and a half and was probably buried in the newly consecrated Jewish cemetery.[10] This was the second child Fanny had lost during her first five years of marriage.

SAN FRANCISCO.

View of San Francisco, California, 1853. Courtesy of the Bancroft Library, University of California, Berkeley.

In 1858 the family moved further away from town life, to the mining camp of Timbuctoo, a short-lived hamlet northeast of Marysville. There in 1859 Fanny gave birth to her fifth child, Eveline, said to be the first white child born there.[11] Julius bought mining claims and opened a store selling miners' clothing, pickaxes, shovels, nails, tobacco, and groceries.[12] After six months of living in a windy three-room shack (the third room being the store), the sick and discouraged family returned to San Francisco, but they did not stay for long. Fanny and Julius soon learned that with the popularity of the route across the Isthmus of Panama, it was now possible for the hardy traveler to go east for a visit.

Although some emigrants never saw their families again, this was not the case for Fanny. During the year when she had journeyed overland, her parents and siblings had immigrated to the United States. Since the transisthmian railroad was now complete, mobile westerners like Fanny and Julius did not feel that their separation from eastern family members was permanent. In 1860 Julius and Fanny and their children traveled for eight weeks by steamship and across the Isthmus of Panama to visit Fanny's parents and siblings in New York. They had been separated for six years. After a six-month visit, the Brookses returned to San Francisco, making the same trip back across the Isthmus.

Despite having friends and relatives nearby, Fanny did not like the fog and cold of the Bay City, so two years later the family moved again. Fanny, Julius, and the young children joined a wagon train of eight for Portland, taking two weeks to travel up the coast. For two years they lived in Portland, as Julius started a store with a Scotsman. The partnership failed, so the family moved again, to Boise, Idaho, then a mining community. This time the family did not even stay a year, as Fanny was subject to high-altitude headaches. Ten years after they left, the family returned to live in Salt Lake City.

In the 1860s Salt Lake City was a wild town, with "drinking, gambling, chewing tobacco, spitting and smoking, and fast women. Men spat as they walked along the street and often the ladies' dresses received the full benefit."[13] The mid-1860s was a boom time for the city and the period when most Jewish merchants settled in the area. It was the era of opportunity for such merchants as the Auerbachs, Ransohoffs, and others who, after a time in the unstable mining towns of the Far West, were hoping to settle down in Salt Lake City, with its steadily growing economy.[14] There, Fanny kept boarders, ran a business, and encouraged her husband to speculate in real estate, as there were many immigrants. Julius became a prosperous merchant and landowner. In addition to suggesting investments for the family from behind the scenes, Fanny often dealt with the public. While Julius could spot fine merchandise and was the buyer for all their retail and wholesale businesses, Fanny drew on her experiences with all kinds of people to make a sale. A successful businesswoman, she amply displayed her ability as a diplomat when, in the late 1870s in her millinery store, she sold several hats to a woman Julius had recently insulted.[15]

Although from that time on Fanny would always consider Salt Lake City her home, the family visited New York, San Francisco, and Europe for significant periods of time. In 1879 Eveline married Sam Auerbach, another Prussian immigrant whose family had also lived in California before settling in Utah.[16] At this time there were estimated to be 180 Jews in Salt Lake City,[17] far fewer than the 16,000 who made up the Jewish community of San Francisco.[18]

In their final years Fanny and Julius, financially secure from their real-estate investments, traveled to Europe on long vacations, enjoying the

Brooks Arcade, Salt Lake City, Utah, early 1900s. Used by permission of the Utah State Historical Society, all rights reserved, photo no. 21683.

resort life of San Remo and Wiesbaden. In 1894, at the age of fifty-six, still wanting to travel, Fanny complained in a letter to an old friend in Salt Lake City, Carlotta Popper, the wife of one of the founders of the city's first synagogue, that she had to spend the winter in Wiesbaden, where her grand-children were in school learn-ing German, rather then traveling on to sunny Italy.[19] Julius died in San Remo in 1891 and Fanny in Wiesbaden in 1901. Both were buried in the Jewish cemetery of Salt Lake City, the same place where Fanny had previously buried another three of her seven children. Only two survived her.[20]

What is significant about Fanny's life, and what does it tell us about western Jewish women? Like her mother-in-law in Silesia, Fanny helped her husband run a store and balance the family's finances. But while her mother-in-law spent most of her life in a village where the family had lived for several generations,[21] Fanny and Julius's stores were in the supply town of Marysville, the transient mining town of Timbuctoo, the river town of Portland, and the young and unstable way station of Salt Lake City. When the business cycle took a downturn, the family moved on or changed businesses. In these towns, most of their customers were not Jewish, and Fanny often had to use all her business sense to keep her Jewish, Mormon, and other customers happy.

In the mining and émigré town of Salt Lake City, a town with more men than women, Fanny, who could not bake as a bride, learned to be an accom-plished cook and took in boarders to supplement the family income. Since most Jewish men were bachelors in the early days of the city, boardinghouses were at a premium. Later, in the 1870s, when Salt Lake City became more established and there were more families, Fanny became a milliner, selling hats to both Jewish and Mormon women. But no matter what business she was engaged in, Fanny held the purse strings, and the Brooks family achieved wealth in part because of her management skills. In Eveline's words, "Mother bought only what we needed."[22] It was Fanny who made the decisions about what property to buy and where to live. It was also Fanny who went to see Brigham Young when there was a conflict between Jewish merchants and the Mormon community. Mormons were forbidden to rent property from "gentiles" such as the Brookses until Fanny convinced Young to change the restrictions.

Although for much of her life Fanny lived in towns without a large Jewish community, she was not isolated from family and friends. Even when in Marysville, her brother Max lived nearby, and Fanny's life was filled with relatives and old acquaintances. While in Salt Lake City, she took part in the city's social events, and she often visited her parents and siblings in New York, once bringing her children for a prolonged visit of five years! However, as much as she traveled, Fanny considered herself a resident of the West, always referring to Salt Lake City as home. When the synagogue was built there in 1890, one photograph was placed in the cornerstone, that of Fanny as the first Jewish woman to settle in the territory.[23]

MARY GOLDSMITH PRAG (1846–1935)
From Calvaria to San Francisco: A Teacher and Activist

A probable acquaintance of Fanny Brooks, Mary Goldsmith Prag also raised children in Utah and there buried a son. However, while Fanny's life was filled with travel, family, and business, Mary's was focused on education and educators. She was recognized as a leader by both the Jewish community and the community at large. Arriving in San Francisco when she was only five years old, she was part of the first generation of Californians as well as of the state's Jewish community. Because most organizations and institutions were young and rapidly growing, Mary, who began as an educator in public and religious schools, was able to quickly rise to positions of leadership in both the Jewish and secular communities. As a Jewish woman in very public roles, she set an example for others to follow.

On 7 July 1852, the crowded steamer SS *Louis* docked off San Francisco, bringing the Goldsmith family to their new home. Traveling with Mary from Calvaria, Poland, were her brother, sister, mother (Sarah), and father (Isaac), a *schohet* (Jewish ritual butcher) for the new Jewish community. After a short stay in New York, they had come west by way of Nicaragua. Mary vividly remembered the crossing:

> We had each and all paid tribute to the Isthmus in the form of 'Chills and Fever,'. . . Part of the journey was to be by land, part by water along the Chagres River. A native had been hired to carry me, but I was fretful and sick, so father placed me before him on the saddle and we jogged along. By water we were transported in canoes through dense masses of verdure which clogged the streams. Most of the time the natives were in the water dragging and pushing the boat along.[24]

OPPOSITE: **Mary Goldsmith Prag, 1864. Courtesy of the Magnes Museum, Berkeley and San Francisco.**

Portraits of Sarah and Isaac Goldsmith, parents of Mary Goldsmith Prag. Courtesy of the Magnes Museum, Berkeley and San Francisco, gift of Mr. and Mrs. Julius Kahn III.

When they arrived in San Francisco, they found a bustling port city sandwiched between hills, sand dunes, and empty fields. In its cosmopolitan atmosphere Mary had the advantage of growing up in a diverse Jewish community and the chance to help shape a new western Jewish life.

In the fall of 1852 Mary attended Rosh Hashanah services at Congregation Sherith Israel. Known as the Polish synagogue, it had been founded a year and a half before by Orthodox Jewish men from England, Poland, and Posen. As in most traditional congregations, men sat on the first floor, women in the gallery above. Mary remembered that "away from family and friends, [men] clung more closely together and were more devoted to the faith of their fathers."[25] One of the men probably present, Conrad Prag, a forty-niner and signatory of the synagogue's constitution, would later become Mary's husband.

When San Francisco acquired its first rabbi, Julius Eckman, in 1854, he established a religious school for children, and Mary was one of his first pupils. In later years, she wrote,

> How we loved our school, how eagerly we hastened there every afternoon.
> How anxiously we looked forward to our Sabbath afternoon services which

64

were regularly held there, and in which we officiated, where with all our souls we sang our 'Shemah Yisroel' and 'Enkelohenu,' our dear Master [Rabbi Eckman] seated at the organ, and then, how we enjoyed the feast of cake and fruit which was sure to follow if we had done well.[26]

As she grew to adulthood, Mary moved from student to teacher in Rabbi Eckman's school. There she received a thorough Jewish education to complement the good secular education she received in the San Francisco public schools. Upon graduation from high school, Mary entered the state Normal School and became a high school teacher as well as religious school teacher.

Soon after the completion of her teaching degree, Mary married Conrad Prag in an 1866 ceremony performed by Rabbi Eckman. Upon their marriage, the nineteen-year-old Mary moved to Salt Lake City, where Conrad was a partner in the firm of Ransohoff & Co., one of the largest merchandise stores in the territory, with a prominent stone building in Salt Lake City.[27] As exemplified by Fanny's life story, it was quite common for Jewish merchants and their wives to move from town to town as economies changed.

During this boom time for Salt Lake City, Mary became familiar with Mormon customs and acquainted with Brigham Young and several of his wives. She wrote about her four years there in a memoir titled "Some Reminiscences of My Life among the Mormons." One of her strongest memories of this time was being asked by Young if she and her husband were Jews "by birth and race, or [were] converts to Judaism." Mary replied, "By birth, race, faith, [and] conviction." Responded Young, "Then you can never become Mormons; no true Jew can be converted to Mormonism."[28] Mary's friendship with Young did not prevent her from voicing her opposition to polygamy and decrying the treatment of Mormon women. She believed that "the desert plains have been watered with women's tears; the desert soil has been nurtured with women's blood; the desert plants have crushed out women's hearts."[29] While in Utah, Mary comforted several Mormon women who were unhappy with their circumstances. Growing up in cosmopolitan San Francisco, she, although always an identified Jew, had friends of many faiths and ethnic backgrounds; with her education and life experience she was well prepared to confidently state her opinions to people from different backgrounds.

In Utah Mary gave birth to two children, Jesse, who died in childhood, and Florence, who grew up to become the first Jewish woman elected to the United States Congress. Active in Utah's small Jewish community, Conrad blew the *shofar* (ram's horn) for the community's 1867 Jewish New Year's service.[30] The Prags moved again in 1869, returning to

Congregation Sherith Israel, Post and Taylor Streets, San Francisco, c. 1900, after facade was refurbished. Courtesy of the Magnes Museum, Berkeley and San Francisco.

San Francisco. They were just one of the many Jewish families who moved back and forth between these two western hubs. In her home city Mary resumed teaching in the religious schools of congregation Sherith Israel and Emanu-El. She became vice principal of Girls' High School and head of its history department.

During these years Mary became a strong voice for the rights of teachers and women. Known as the "Mother of the Pension Movement in California," she fought for a teachers' pension bill, stating at an 1892 meeting of the California State Teachers' Association, "We claim that it is the duty of the State to pension and care for our teachers—they who train our rising generation to become good men and women, and good citizens."[31] She also advocated vacation pay and tenure for educators, the permanent recording of their certificates, and the enforcement of a law that prescribed equal pay for male and female instructors. Not surprisingly, she headed a group of teachers who defeated a proposal by the Board of Education that would have excluded married women from the field. These bills were personally important to her, since she would continue as a teacher and administrator at Girls' High School until she was well into her seventies. Jewish and gentile women and men alike benefited from her work, and she was recognized as a pioneering educator by both communities.

Beyond defending the rights of teachers, Mary was a supporter of women's suffrage, participating in the 1894, 1895, and 1896 Women's Congresses held in San Francisco. At the 1896 meeting, she presented a paper entitled "The State," which extolled the virtues of modern democratic government. To culminate her career, Mary was the first Jewish woman appointed to the San Francisco Board of Education, occupying one of the two newly created "Jewish seats."[32] To reduce Catholic influence, the board was reorganized in 1921, with Catholics, Protestants, Labor, and

Florence and Jessie Prag, children of Mary and Conrad Prag, 1872. Courtesy of the Magnes Museum, Berkeley and San Francisco.

Jews each having representation. A prerequisite for Mary's appointment was leadership in the Jewish community. She demonstrated this through her memberships in the Jewish Educational Society, Jewish Community Center, and Federation of Jewish Charities as well as in other Jewish religious and community organizations. When appointed, she was seventy-five; she was later reappointed with the strong support of San Francisco teachers and served until her death at age eighty-nine. This final public appointment of Mary's career was the melding of the two themes of her life: the Jewish community and education. It further exemplified how an immigrant Jewish woman in the West could feel equally at home in both the Jewish and secular worlds.

This remarkable person is extremely important for any study of western women because her prominence as a Jewish woman was only one facet of her life. Raised in an observant home, as a child she attended services at the first two congregations in San Francisco, Sherith Israel and Emanu-El. Her short memoir provides one of the few first-person accounts of growing up in San Francisco during the turbulent 1850s and 1860s, with vigilantism and the boom-and-bust economy. Her later memories of life in the Mormon town of Salt Lake City demonstrate the limited access and the barriers that existed between Mormons and "gentiles." Because of her friendship with the Mormon leadership, Mary was able to gain entrée to private homes, and her ability as an author led to the recording of Mormon women's lives.

Moreover, as an activist, Mary left speeches that document her work as an educator and a fighter for the rights of women and teachers. In this way she served as a leader of the Jewish community and of the general community. In many of her talks she used Jewish imagery, quoting, for example, from the Ethics of the Fathers and the Bible to emphasize her points. This form of Jewish reference was followed by her daughter, Florence Prag Kahn of San Francisco, the first Jewish congresswoman.

FLORA LANGERMANN SPIEGELBERG
(1857–1943)
From New York to Santa Fe: A Community Leader

Working on the local level in the Southwest, Flora Langermann Spiegelberg supported both Jewish and community-wide projects, working with Jews and non-Jews to establish Jewish community institutions and helping to improve the urban environment. Mobility and adaptability to new places characterized the first half of her life. Born in New York City in 1857, she was taken by her mother to San Francisco when she was just two months old. Flora's maternal grandfather, Moses Lichtenheim, had come to New York from Hamburg in 1820, while her maternal grandmother was a non-Jew and American-born, tracing her ancestry back to colonial-period Hessians.[33] Flora's father, Colonel William Langermann, a native of Bavaria, had been an officer of the California State Militia. After nine years in gold rush San Francisco, the family returned to New York City by way of the Isthmus of Panama.

In 1869, on the death of the colonel, Flora's mother again took her on a long journey, this time to Nuremberg, a leading city in Bavaria, so that she would receive a good education. Five years later, when Flora was seventeen, she met and married Willi Spiegelberg. He had left Germany when he was fifteen, and after spending a year working in New York, he joined his brothers in their Southwest store.[34] At age thirty, Willi, already a success in New Mexico, had returned to Germany to visit family and friends. When asked why she married him, Flora responded, "I was young and he was handsome."[35] The Spiegelbergs were the first couple married in the new Nuremberg Reform Temple, an impressive structure consecrated on Hans Sachs Square in 1874.

After a luxury wedding trip to the capitals of Europe in 1875, Flora accompanied her husband to her new home in Santa Fe, becoming one of the first Jewish women to take the Santa Fe Trail. The trip and her introduction to the Southwest were quite eye-opening for her, as New Mexico had little in common with San Francisco, New York, or Nuremberg, the places of her youth. Indeed, the Nuremberg that Flora left had a Jewish population of about 3,000. Flora and Willi took the steam train as far southwest as it went, to Las Animas, Colorado. There they spent the night in a ramshackle hotel that looked like "large packing cases." According to Flora, they were greeted by 200 cowboys who had just returned from a roundup and had not seen a woman in months. Frightened, Flora spent the night wearing all her clothes in a room that was "partitioned off with thin all revealing muslin."[36] In the morning they boarded a four-horse stagecoach. It stopped at log house coach stations three times a day for an hour to change horses and for its occupants to eat. Years later, Flora could still describe the menu: "dried buffalo chips, with beans, red or green peppers,

Five Spiegelberg brothers: left to right, Willi, Emanuel, S. J., Levi, Lehman, c. 1865–70. Courtesy of the Museum of New Mexico, Santa Fe. Photo by Sarony, neg. no. 11025.

coffee and tea without milk or sugar, and occasional delicacies such as buffalo tongues, bear and buffalo steaks."[37] Riding over the rocky and dusty roads, it took them six long days to reach the outskirts of Santa Fe.

When Flora arrived there, Santa Fe had been home to the five Spiegelberg brothers for over thirty years. Willi was the youngest. Since 1844, when the eldest brother, Solomon Jacob Spiegelberg, first came to Santa Fe from Bavaria, the brothers, all in their late teens when they arrived in New Mexico, were merchants, doing business with locals, Indians, and the United States Army. Beginning as retailers of groceries and dry goods, they expanded to become wholesalers.[38] Soon after the American takeover of New Mexico in 1846, the Spiegelbergs had one of the largest mercantile enterprises in the territory, supplying the troops with local and eastern products.[39] In 1872 they established the Second National Bank of New Mexico and played a role in mining and real estate.

As the community of Jewish businessmen rose to thirty-two in 1860,

69

Engagement photo of Willi (Wolf) Spiegelberg, 1873. Courtesy of his great-granddaughter Sue R. Warburg, San Francisco.

Old Adobe Palace, Santa Fe (now Palace of the Governors), c. 1881. Courtesy of the Museum of New Mexico, Santa Fe. Photo by Ben Wittick, neg. no. 15.

the foundations of a Jewish community were laid. Although the community was still mostly comprised of young unmarried German-born men, there were now six Jewish families in New Mexico.[40] This same year, the first Yom Kippur observance took place in Santa Fe, at the home of Levi Spiegelberg.[41] A decade later almost one-third of the men were married, and children were becoming more numerous. In 1875, the year Flora reached Santa Fe, a doctor was brought from Colorado to perform two circumcisions, and in 1876 the first bar mitzvah ceremony took place in the city.[42] By 1878 there were thought to be 108 Jews in Santa Fe.[43]

Having spent her early years in the United States and teen years in Europe, Flora was well prepared to provide leadership for both the Jewish and general communities. Even as a new immigrant, she was fluent in English and accustomed to a multiethnic social life. Until Flora arranged for the building of a two-room, nonsectarian school in 1879, the Catholic Church controlled all the schools in Santa Fe.[44] In 1882 she started a Sabbath school for Jewish children, and many of the city's Jewish religious ceremonies were held in her home. Socializing beyond the Jewish community, Flora became friends with governmental and religious leaders. For example, she was a confidant of Archbishop Jean Baptiste Lamy and was proud of the good relations that existed between the Jews and Catholics of Santa Fe.

In the 1880s Flora's home on Palace Avenue was the first residence in Santa Fe to have running water and gas appliances. When her husband became mayor of Santa Fe in 1880, Flora became the town's hostess, entertaining Americans and local wealthy families with elaborate dinners, complete with fine wines served by attendants and classical piano played by the hostess herself. However, by 1890 she sought a wider Jewish community and better educational opportunities for her two children. Willi retired from the family business, and they moved east. Returning to New York, Flora became a Progressive Age reformer, working to remove garbage from the streets of New York, and an author, writing articles for adults and stories for children about her life in New Mexico.

Although Flora spent only fifteen years there, her achievements lived on in Santa Fe. Others would continue the Jewish services and Sabbath school she established, and she would be credited as one of the founders of Jewish community life. In some western towns with small Jewish communities, a person's length of residence was not always as important as what they accomplished and how they led their lives while they were a community member.

LEAH LANDMAN
(1867–unknown)
From a Russian Village to the Wyoming Prairie: A Farm Wife and a Mother

Leah Landman lived for seventeen years on the Wyoming prairie; her biography represents another part of the story of Jewish women in the West. Attracted by open farming land, not mineral or mercantile riches, some Jewish men and women raised their families on the western prairies. While Flora Langermann Spiegelberg was in New York writing stories of her New Mexico life, Leah was reaching adulthood in a small town near Odessa, Russia, where she was engaged to Simon Landman, a farmer who was renting land to grow corn and melons. The couple planned to be married when they reached America. Simon was fearful that if they married in Russia, they would never leave. Leah's story of separation, business hardships, and motivation to educate her children is a typical, almost stereotypical, telling of the narrative of Jewish life in the United States. Where Leah's tale differs from the standard was in her husband's strong desire to own land and to farm.

In 1887 Leah, Simon, and his sister Deborah crossed the border into Austria; there they separated, afraid to look like an emigrant group, as emigration without proper papers was outlawed. When they reunited down the road, they decided that because their funds were insufficient to allow all three of them to go to New York, Simon would depart directly for the United States while Leah and Deborah would travel to England.

With no friends or relatives in London, the women were not permitted to go ashore until a representative from a shelter for girls took responsibility for them. In London, living at the shelter, the women worked until they had enough money to go on to America. London was often a temporary stop for Jewish immigrants to the United States. There they learned English and observed unfamiliar customs. This experience would help them when they reached American shores. During her nine months in London, Leah witnessed Queen Victoria's Jubilee celebration, the queen and elaborate procession making a lifelong impression on her. In the stories of her childhood, queens were tall and stately. In Leah's mind the slight Victoria did not have the correct appearance of a queen.

When she had sufficient funds, Leah set off on her own for America, Deborah having decided to remain in London. Traveling in steerage, Leah was sick most of the way. At the voyage's end, she encountered a new set of problems. Being unfamiliar with the immigration process, she was unaware that she would have to prove to immigration officials that she had adequate funds to support herself during her first days in her new country. A German couple befriended her, gave her money, and put her on a train to Pittsburgh, where she finally was reunited with Simon. Leah was also greeted by relatives, who provided her with a place to live until she and Simon were married in 1899.

Initially the Landmans worked in a cigar factory; after many long days, they managed to save enough to purchase a milk-delivery business. Buying milk from the dairy, Simon would deliver it throughout the neighborhoods of Pittsburgh, transporting it by horse and wagon. In 1900 Leah gave birth to the first of her thirteen children. By the time that she had three children, she was ready for a change. The dairy was not doing well. There was much talk of "free land" in the West, and Simon went off to Wyoming to inspect homestead property. What he found was barren earth, with only tall grass and open prairies. He did not file a claim, as he believed that his wife "would not like this overwhelming land."[45] However, as he wanted to become a farmer, he decided to buy property in Pennsylvania. With his wife's blessing he made a bid on the land. Unfortunately, the sale was fraudulent, so they returned to Pittsburgh. By this time they had to find a new way to make a living. The dairy business was failing, as most small delivery companies were, because of competition from larger operations. Simon sold what he could and again went out to Wyoming. This time he traveled with others to land near Torrington. There, in 1906, he staked his claim with five other Jewish men from Pittsburgh.[46] The Homestead Act allowed settlers to acquire 160 acres as long as they developed the property and built homes.

Soon there were close to sixty families in the Torrington area.[47] Some came for the free land and the chance to work for themselves, while others were socialists, hoping to get away from the capitalism of the cities and live on the land. Especially before World War I, Wyoming welcomed foreign-born settlers, believing that they would become an asset to the state. Indeed, the commissioner of immigration for Wyoming enthusiastically advertised the state to Russian Jews.[48] The Wyoming settlement was the idea of Rabbi Leonard Levy, who persuaded the Jewish Agricultural Society to help fourteen families settle on the land. In this time of talk of immigration quotas, Levy believed that "it is not restriction that we need . . . but proper distribution we require."[49] For the Landmans, moving to Wyoming was a personal decision, not part of a grand resettlement program—Simon just wanted to farm. This was not a new occupation for him or his family, but one they had followed in Europe for several generations on leased land.

In February 1907, when Simon returned to Pittsburgh to take his family to their new home, Leah still did not want to go to Wyoming. She had hoped that her husband would change his mind. "But as Father" was "in love with Wyoming," wrote his daughter Minnie in her autobiography, there was no chance of that. Minnie believed that "the heady feeling of freedom had done something for [him]. He fretted at living in the city and hurried to make preparations for departure."[50] Then the Landman family "took the train to the Promised Land."[51] Coincidentally, this land was not far from the wagon trail that had brought Fanny Brooks to the West more than fifty years earlier; in fact, it was near the place where she had lost her first child. At this time there were 300 Jews living in all of Wyoming.[52]

When they reached Torrington and took a carriage out to the prairie, Minnie described her mother as sitting silently, "enveloped in gloom. The landscape, what was visible of it, depressed her."[53] However, her mood lightened a bit when neighbors greeted her. Most were from Pittsburgh, and she had known some of them previously. Leah faced many hardships in setting up a home in Wyoming. While most of the other settlers built sod or dugout homes, Simon built a large, two-room house of lumber. Although it looked grand on the prairie, it was subject to the area's wild winds and was extremely hard to heat. As Minnie later wrote, "[W]e nearly froze in 'elegance.'"[54] Until a well was dug, water had to be hauled four miles from a shallow stream. All the furniture sent from Pittsburgh was damaged, mirrors were broken, and all china was in pieces. "My mother who had not said one word against the grim land to which she had come unwillingly wept for hours," Minnie recalled. "[A]s mother was expecting a child in July father became alarmed at her crying so hard."[55]

For Leah, being a farm wife meant helping with all the work, including building fences, cooking, and covering for her husband when he was away, as he often took short jobs in Nebraska to make money in the slow seasons. During this time the one thing that she really wanted was a cow. It took a while, but finally she got one, and her children had milk.

Like Flora Langermann Spiegelberg, isolated in New Mexico, Leah's main concern was that her offspring receive a good education. Before settling in Wyoming, she had enrolled her older children in school in Pittsburgh. She was well aware of the results a good education could bring. However, the school "year" on the prairie was only eight weeks in the summer of 1907, and there was no school building; the children later met in the home of Charlie Cohen, a settler who arrived with his family in 1908.[56] Wanting a school of their own, the community of farmers sent a representative to the school board in Torrington. The board only told them that they would "think about it." At first, the community had little recourse, as the immigrants did not know how to force the school board to act. Eventually, Leah, worried that her children were growing up "like wild Indians," took matters into her own hands and went to the school board, and they finally agreed to send a teacher the following year.[57] In addition, the school board gave the community lumber for a schoolhouse but told them that they had to build it themselves. A one-room structure known as the Jewish school was built in 1908. In 1912 the school board promised them a term of a few months, but Leah was still unsatisfied with the level of education. Her daughter commented, "Mother, who never did like Wyoming, was constantly bewailing the fact that [her children] were growing up in worse ignorance than children in Russia."[58]

The school board did not feel obligated to help the new Jewish settlers. Although they at times appointed qualified teachers, they also chose individuals who were anti-Semitic. One such educator asked the class how Jews butchered animals. When a student replied, the teacher told the children that that was a "wicked" way to kill animals.[59] The instructor then beat the pupil and said, "[W]hat can you expect from Christ killers anyway?"[60] Because this happened while most of the men were away from their farms, working in Nebraska, the women of the community started a petition drive to dismiss the teacher. Leah signed the petition for her family; it was not that easy, however, to have a teacher fired. Although some Wyoming officials were seeking foreign immigrants, others in the state were sympathetic to the growing national xenophobia and the call for immigration restrictions.

Although a secular education was hard to come by, at times the children did receive a religious education. The family and most of the settlers maintained Orthodox Jewish beliefs. Religious services were held in homes and the school on High Holidays, and a Torah was purchased in

Pittsburgh and brought to the prairie.[61] During the winters, Simon taught his children Hebrew at home. In the fall of 1908 the community brought a rabbi from Pittsburgh out to Wyoming, and he filed a claim for land. They built him a house and pledged to support him and his family. This arrangement was short-lived, though, as the rabbi's wife did not like Wyoming. Before he returned to Pittsburgh, however, he allowed the Landman children to study with him. Several families sent their boys to this prairie "cheder." Because the Landmans' son was afraid of crossing the prairie alone, two of their daughters accompanied him and also studied. All spring and summer the children practiced their lessons at the rabbi's home, as there was no secular school that year. Later, when a second rabbi settled in the area, the children would do their farm chores and then walk a half-mile to the rabbi's house to study. There they would complete their schoolwork and study Hebrew.[62]

When Minnie graduated from high school at age eighteen in 1920, she was hired to teach at her former one-room school.[63] She only taught one year, however, as Leah and Simon thought that she was required to do too much work for too little pay. There were few opportunities for adult children in the Torrington area. When Leah heard that her sister and sister's family, who had also farmed in Wyoming, were happy in Nebraska, she insisted on leaving. After seventeen years on the prairie, the family left the farm for Omaha. Many of Leah's friends and family members were already living in this city, which had a well-established Jewish community and a Jewish population of more than ten thousand.[64] However, according to Minnie, "now father was unhappy and mother wasn't happy either. Through all the ups and downs of life on the prairies my mother had the prettiest complexion and pink cheeks. Her hair was jet black and I always thought she was the prettiest woman alive. . . . [S]he had not been in town six months when her hair began to turn gray and her face lost all its color, she became pale and looked worried constantly."[65]

In spite of her dislike for Omaha, this ended Leah's travels, and the Landmans would become a part of the growing community there. This was the third location Leah would call home since she had left her birthplace of Russia. Pittsburgh, the Wyoming farm, and now the city of Omaha all affected her view of American life and the West. Having no permanent roots, Leah's older children went off on their own; only the younger ones made Omaha their home.

The Landmans had stayed on the prairie longer than most. The dry land did not have a sufficient water supply and could not support family farming.[66] Many settlers only stayed the five years necessary to own their homesteaded land; then they sold it and moved on.[67] Relocating until they reached a city they could call home—this was a necessary part of western Jewish history for many families.

Conclusion

The West is a varied landscape with many regional differences; the Jewish West is even more complex. Many Jewish women considered Jewish community life to be essential. Besides seeing it as a place to make friends and as a center of Jewish observance, women usually sought Jewish community life for schooling and marriage partners for their children. Raised in a strong Jewish community in San Francisco and educated in good Jewish and secular schools, Mary Goldsmith Prag would choose to raise her daughter in this cosmopolitan city. There, her daughter, Florence Prag Kahn, would attain a Jewish education, attend the University of California at Berkeley, marry a Jewish congressman, Julius Kahn, and successfully run for the United States Congress in her own right. Mary's daughter was raised in a city where Jews were seven to eight percent of the total population.[68] Fanny Brooks and Flora Langermann Spiegelberg faced different situations. They sought to give their children a Jewish and secular education, but because the small Jewish communities in Salt Lake City and Santa Fe lacked good schools, the women chose to educate their children in New York and Europe. However, both Flora and Fanny always held on to their western identities. Even in the twentieth century, Leah Landman faced the same problem on the prairies of Wyoming. Although life was hard and money scarce, one of her main concerns was that her children attain a good education. She did not have the possibility of moving elsewhere; she had to fight for her children's needs where she had settled. In the West, where Jews were often a minority, Jewish women were likely to forge relationships with non-Jews. On the prairie, Leah Landman had to approach the non-Jewish residents of Torrington so that her children would have teachers and a school.

Like the United States as a whole, the West was a land of migrants. Because of mineral rushes, boom-and-bust economies, and free land, many cultures and ethnic groups in the West shared the same paths to economic and social opportunities. In multiethnic San Francisco, Mary Goldsmith Prag gained from her relationship with the Unitarian minister Thomas Starr King and filled the Jewish seat on the city's board of education. During her years in Salt Lake City, Mary learned how to work with Mormons. Fanny Brooks had to learn about Mormon society too, at one time

going to Brigham Young to lobby for the right to rent to Mormons. She also was exposed to Chinese culture by a family that rented property from them. In Santa Fe, Flora Langermann Spiegelberg entertained dignitaries, including President and Mrs. Rutherford B. Hayes and General William Tecumseh Sherman, and worked with Protestant clergy to establish a nonparochial school.

Most Jewish women in the West had to accept mobility and change. Some had lived in the eastern United States or in England before traveling on; therefore, they were already familiar with the language and culture and were less green by the time they reached the West.

Because of the transportation revolution of the mid-nineteenth century and the various economic upheavals and mineral rushes, women, like men, were able to travel from their ancestral homes to new lives in America. Often they moved many times using a variety of modes of transportation; once an initial trip was made, it was easier to pick up and relocate once more. Fanny Brooks, in her remarkable life, traveled from her home near Breslau to New York by ship, then by train to Nebraska, and then by wagon train to California. After a year in California she went by steamer and crossed the Isthmus of Panama, next taking another steamer to New York, where she visited with her parents for a few months. She then made the return trip to California and within a year traveled by wagon train to Portland and then back to Salt Lake City. This was all before she reached the age of thirty. Later in life she would travel by train to New York for extended visits and then vacation in Europe, traveling by luxury ship. Flora Langermann Spiegelberg, born in New York, also would travel throughout the West and return to New York. Mary Goldsmith Prag, after reaching California by steamship as a child, would travel to Salt Lake City to be a merchant's wife and in later life attend a meeting of the American Historical Association in Rhode Island and visit her daughter in Washington, D.C. Leah Landman, after crossing the border of Russia, lived for nine months in London before going by ship to New York, by train to Pittsburgh, then settling on the prairies of Wyoming, and after seventeen years there finally moving to Omaha.

Although both Jewish men and women often moved from place to place in Europe for business or marriage pursuits, the mobility of Jews in the American West was particularly striking.[69] Boom-and-bust cycles affected mining-town economies, and the advent of the railroad often changed settlement patterns. Not only did these women travel to visit or to settle permanently, they often moved back and forth between isolated communities and major cities, staying for months or a few years, a pattern that was not found in the older Jewish communities of the East, where movement to a new home was usually a one-way trip across town.

What does this all say about future generations of Jewish women in the West? While their new lives were not always filled with the milk and honey of the Promised Land, for some, especially those who settled in the cities, the identification with place was strong. Despite the fact that she spent considerable time in New York and Europe, Fanny Brooks considered Salt Lake City her home, as did her daughter Eveline Auerbach. The identities of Mary Goldsmith Prag and her daughter Florence Prag Kahn as Jewish women, as founders of state and local institutions, and as role models for Jewish and non-Jewish women are without equal. Even today the family of Flora Langermann Spiegelberg, although her time in Santa Fe was only fifteen years, still feels that the western experience is a part of their heritage. And while farming did not stay in the Landman family, for Leah's daughter Minnie the experience of being raised on the prairie with inadequate schools made her want to be a teacher and educate others.

As the fields of women's history and American Jewish history expand, the lives of Fanny Brooks, Mary Goldsmith Prag, Flora Langermann Spiegelberg, and Leah Landman, along with the lives of other women who spent years in mining towns, frontier cities, and on the prairie, will join the histories of Jewish women in the labor movement, in radical politics, and on the stage to present a complete history of the era.[70] Moreover, when historians fully tell the story of Jewish life in the West, these women and others like them will play an important role in redefining American Jewish history.

NOTES

1. Minnie Landman DeNelsky, "An Autobiography" (Cincinnati: American Jewish Archives, n.d.), 70.

2. See *The Jewish Woman in America* (New York: Dial Press, 1976). The coauthors, Charlotte Baum, Paula Hyman, and Sonya Michel, who pioneered the field, consider western Jewish women as part of their study. See also Jacob Rader Marcus, *The American Jewish Woman: A Documentary History* (Cincinnati: American Jewish Archives, 1981), and *The American Jewish Woman, 1654–1980* (Cincinnati: American Jewish Archives, 1981), and especially the monumental *Jewish Women in America* (New York: Routledge, 1997), two volumes edited by Paula E. Hyman and Deborah Dash Moore that include western women.

3. Harriet Lane Levy, *920 O'Farrell Street: A Jewish Girlhood in Old San Francisco* (Berkeley: Heyday Books, 1996); Sophie Trupin, *Dakota Diaspora: Memoirs of a Jewish Homesteader* (Berkeley: Alternative Press, 1984); Linda Mack Schloff, *And Prairie Dogs Weren't Kosher: Jewish Women in the Upper Midwest since 1855* (Saint Paul: Minnesota Historical Society Press, 1996).

4. Alfred Julius Bruck, "The Bruck Family: A Historical Sketch of a Jewish Family through a Thousand Years," *Historia Judaica* 9, no. 2 (1947).

5. Annegret S. Ogden, *Frontier Reminiscences of Eveline Brooks Auerbach* (Berkeley: Friends of the Bancroft Library), 22. One version of the manuscript suggests that an uncle marrying a niece was a problem, but that it was soon worked out.

6. An early draft of the memoir reads, "The children had been given a good education, something unusual for Jews even in those days as only few Jews were allowed in schools." Eveline Brooks Auerbach, second draft of memoir (Bancroft Library, Berkeley), 1.

7. Eveline Auerbach collection, 92/757, Bancroft Library, University of California, Berkeley.

8. *History of Yuba County California with Illustrations, Descriptive of Its Scenery, Residences, Public Buildings, Fire Blocks and Manufactories* (Oakland: Thompson and West, 1879), 62.

9. *Marysville Weekly California Express*, 25 October 1856, 4.

10. Few of the stones are still intact, and many are weatherbeaten and unreadable. Many children died in infancy and were buried in the cemetery; however, few markers remain. For more about the cemetery, see Susan Morris, *A Traveler's Guide to Pioneer Jewish Cemeteries of the California Gold Rush* (Berkeley: Magnes Museum, 1996).

11. One version of the town's history states that it was founded by a black miner. See Erwin G. Gudde, *California Place Names* (Berkeley: University of California Press, 1962), 321.

12. Ogden, *Frontier Reminiscences*, 39.

13. Ibid., 47.

14. Leon L. Watters, "The Pioneer Jews of Utah," *Studies in American Jewish History*, no. 2 (1952): 46.

15. Ogden, *Frontier Reminiscences*, 86.

16. Sam Auerbach and his brothers Fred and Theodore operated stores in California and Nevada mining towns before settling in Salt Lake City, where they became merchants and founders of a department store chain that bore their name. Active in the Jewish community, Sam was a founding member and the 1884 president of B'nai Israel Congregation. See *Utah Pioneer Merchant: The Memoirs of Samuel H. Auerbach* (Berkeley: Bancroft Library, 1998), and Harriet Rochlin and Fred Rochlin, *Pioneer Jews: A New Life in the Far West* (Boston: Houghton Mifflin Company, 1984): 109–12.

17. Jacob Rader Marcus, *To Count a People: American Jewish Population Data, 1585–1984* (Lanham, Md.: University Press of America, 1990), 218.

18. Ibid., 28.

19. Eveline Auerbach collection, 92/757, Bancroft Library, University of California, Berkeley.

20. Her son George (1857–68) was the second burial in the Jewish cemetery; the land had been donated in 1866 by Brigham Young.

21. Bruck, "The Bruck Family."

22. Ogden, *Frontier Reminiscences*, 91.

23. Watters, "The Pioneer Jews of Utah," 84.

24. Mary Prag, "Early Days" (Florence Prag Kahn Collection, Western Jewish History Center, Judah L. Magnes Museum, Berkeley), 1.

25. Ibid.

26. Jacob Voorsanger, *The Chronicles of Emanu-El*, xx.

27. For more about Nicholas Ransohoff, see Watters, "The Pioneer Jews of Utah."

28. Mary Prag, "Some Reminiscences of My Life among the Mormons" (Florence Prag Kahn Collection, Western Jewish History Center, Judah L. Magnes Museum, Berkeley), 20.

29. Ibid., 30.

30. Watters, "The Pioneer Jews of Utah," 68.

31. Mary Prag, "Should the State Pension Teachers? An Address Delivered at the California State Teachers' Association" (San Francisco: Frank Eastman & Co., Printers, 1892).

32. David G. Dalin, "Jewish and Non-Partisan Republicanism in San Francisco, 1911–1963," in *The Jews of the West: The Metropolitan Years*, ed. Moses Rischin (Waltham, Mass.: American Jewish Historical Society, 1979), 128.

33. Pauline Kronman, "Meet This Great-Grand-Ma: Introducing Flora Spiegelberg—Under Whose Gray Hair There Are No Sere Brain Creases," *The American Hebrew*, 22 July 1927.

34. Michael L. Lawson, "Flora Langermann Spiegelberg," *Western States Jewish Historical Quarterly* (July 1976): 295.

35. Kronman, "Meet This Great-Grand-Ma."

36. Ibid.

37. Flora Spiegelberg, "Reminiscences of a Jewish Bride of the Santa Fe Trail," *The Jewish Spectator* (August 1937): 21.

38. Floyd S. Fierman, "The Speigelbergs of New Mexico: Merchants and Bankers, 1844–1893." *Southwestern Studies* 1, no. 4 (winter 1964): 15.

39. Henry J. Tobias, *A History of the Jews in New Mexico* (Albuquerque: University of New Mexico Press, 1990), 34.

40. Ibid., 40.

41. Ibid., 42.

42. Ibid., 58.

43. Marcus, *To Count a People*, 137.

44. Flora Spiegelberg, letter to the editor of the *Albuquerque Journal*, 3 January 1939, MSS 18:1, Center for Southwest Research, University of New Mexico.

45. DeNelsky, "An Autobiography," 60.

46. Amy Shapiro, *A Guide to the Jewish Rockies* (Denver: Rocky Mountain Jewish Historical Society, 1979).

47. Ibid.

48. Lawrence A. Cardoso, "Nativism in Wyoming 1868 to 1930: Changing Perceptions of Foreign Immigrants," *Annals of Wyoming* (spring 1986): 26.

49. Carl V. Hallberg, "Jews in Wyoming," *Annals of Wyoming* 61, no. 1 (1989): 17.

50. DeNelsky, "An Autobiography," 67.

51. Ibid., 70.

52. Marcus, *To Count a People*, 236.

53. DeNelsky, "An Autobiography," 72.

54. Ibid., 60.

55. Ibid., 76.

56. Frank Fieldman, "Jewish Settlement of Huntly, Wyoming," 12 January 1968, typescript, 3, Homesteaders Museum, Torrington, Wyoming.

57. Simon believed that the school board hoped the Jews would leave. See DeNelsky, "An Autobiography," 99, 193.

58. Ibid., 128.

59. This is a reference to kosher laws; it demonstrates that these Wyoming Jews were an observant community.

60. DeNelsky, "An Autobiography," 193.

61. Fieldman, "Jewish Settlement of Huntly, Wyoming," 3.

62. The "rabbi" may have been Shmuel Krone, a teacher and ritual slaughterer who lived on a homestead for a few months. His wife's cousin was an early homesteader. See: Shmuel Krone, YIVØ 41, translated from the Yiddish by Daniel Soyer, YIVO Archives, New York.

63. The Torrington school board advised her to seek a teaching position at a school outside their district and to hide her Judaism. They did not want to hire a Jewish teacher. However, she held them to a former promise. They told her that she could not handle the "tough" pupils, who included her brothers and sisters and new Russian immigrants. See DeNelsky, "An Autobiography," 146.

64. Marcus, *To Count a People*, 118.

65. DeNelsky, "An Autobiography," 163.

66. Sally Vanderpoel, "Jewish Agricultural Society Experiment in Eastern Wyoming, 1906–1918," *Annals of Wyoming* (summer 1997): 3.

67. Shapiro, *A Guide to the Jewish Rockies*.

68. Moses Rischin and John Livingston, eds., *Jews of the American West* (Detroit: Wayne State University Press, 1991), 34.

69. Ellen Eisenberg reinforced my thinking on this point.

70. Two recent important works are Susan A. Glenn, *Daughters of the Shtetl: Life and Labor in the Immigrant Generation* (Ithaca: Cornell University Press, 1990), and Joyce Antler, *The Journey Home: Jewish Women and the American Century* (New York: The Free Press, 1997).

The Jewish Merchant and Civic Order in the Urban West

William Toll

Introduction: Jewish Roles and Images in the American West

I N THE AMERICAN WEST from the California gold rush through the San Francisco earthquake, the Jewish merchant in his brick store on Main Street became a symbol of economic stability and civic pride. In the 1850s in northern California's frenetic mining region, Jewish merchants played a key role as provisioners and exchange agents. They dominated the sale of clothing, dry goods, tobacco, and liquors, which the miners acquired in exchange for gold dust and nuggets and even for stock in small mining ventures. The gold was sent to uncles and older brothers in the regional metropolis of San Francisco, from which the network of supplies and credit radiated.[1] By the 1870s, the Main Streets of Trinidad, Colorado; Prescott, Arizona; Virginia City, Nevada; Albany, Oregon; and Tacoma, Washington, all held clusters of Jewish stores selling the usual dry goods and provisions, while other Jews offered services as tailors, barbers, watchmakers, and saloon keepers. In Santa Fe, the Spiegelberg brothers bought produce, sheep, and cattle from farmers and ranchers and sold them to the U.S. Army and to Indian pueblos and reservations.[2]

For Jewish men, the merchant role in the American West enabled them and their families in a single generation to move from medieval artisanship and itinerant merchandising to the highest civic status. Where else in the world could they have achieved not only economic security but also political leadership and the moral stature of pioneers?[3] A few Jewish merchants with the daring to risk capital in more speculative ventures

Levi Strauss & Co. headquarters, Battery Street, San Francisco, 1880s. From the Archives of *Western States Jewish History.*

Sands Brothers, Jewish merchants in the commercial arcade of Helena, Montana. From the Archives of *Western States Jewish History*.

became financial anchors in the largest urban centers. Men like I. W. Hellman in Los Angeles and Bailey Gatzert in Seattle began as merchants but expanded their investments, earning a reputation among gentile civic leaders as "the most public-spirited men in the place."[4] Hellman, after clerking with an uncle in the 1860s, had by 1872 formed a partnership with John G. Downey, a gentile land speculator, to create the Merchants & Farmers Bank, which bought gold nuggets and grains in exchange for its own circulating notes.[5] During a financial panic in 1877, while Hellman was vacationing in Europe, Downey closed the bank. Hurrying back, Hellman borrowed funds from contacts in San Francisco to reopen the bank and soon bought out Downey. Although he moved to San Francisco in 1890 to become managing partner of the Wells Fargo Bank, Hellman retained business contacts in Los Angeles. With Henry Huntington and others, he invested in the interurban streetcar lines that would turn the Los Angeles basin into a vast real estate speculation.[6]

In the Pacific Northwest, Gatzert became a key promoter of his new city. Arriving in Seattle in 1869 to serve as resident partner of San Francisco's Schwabacher & Company, he invested his profits in new services and industries. In 1881 he organized the Spring Hill Water Company, which built a reservoir and piping system to supply the city's drinking water. In 1883 he started the Puget Sound National Bank of Seattle, which provided credit for the many small operators who developed a vital new industry, the Newcastle coal mines. Gatzert served a term as mayor in the late 1870s, but his energy was primarily projected into the Chamber of Commerce, which he served as president until his death in 1891.[7] The Board of Education thought enough of Gatzert to name a school in his memory; it still exists in a modern structure in the heart of what had been a district of Jewish, Italian, and Japanese immigrants.[8]

Growing up among San Francisco's secure merchant families in the

1880s, Harriet Lane Levy best captured the male persona in this new Jewish culture. She observed:

> All the men were united by the place and circumstance of their birth. They had come to America from villages in Germany, and had worked themselves up from small stores in the interior of California to businesses in San Francisco. . . . There was no deviation from the one standard of excellence. Each had a paying business, a house and lot, and some money in the bank. Each stood firm on his feet, looked the world straight in the eye, and knew that he measured up well by the standard of God and man.[9]

But how had this new self-assurance been created? Why had they as youths had the confidence to leave the villages of Central Europe and travel thousands of miles to the sparsely populated deserts, mountains, and forests of the American West? Although they were a small minority, how had they come to play such vital economic roles as the region's resources were drawn into America's rapidly growing market economy? How had they created families in such widely dispersed towns? How had these sons of Europe's pariahs managed to emerge as civic leaders in the new land?

Jewish Migration from the Peasant World

Students of American Jewish history often see the emigration of young men from the German states as a unique break from a past of village insularity. But historians of modern Europe now see migration in the nineteenth century, both within Europe and overseas, as the extension of choices exercised by peasant families for centuries to enhance their security. Scholars identify four migratory patterns, which they designate as local, circulatory, chain, and career. From the seventeenth century through the 1820s, migration usually was either local or circulatory. Young women sought work for several years prior to marriage as servants in small towns or as textile workers in rural mills. Young men were more likely to migrate seasonally to work as farmhands or construction workers before circulating home for the winter. From the 1830s through the 1890s, however, unprecedented population growth, enclosure of pastureland to grow food crops for city residents, the withdrawal of capital from rural textile mills, and new investment in urban factories, all accelerated by the expanding railroad networks, increased pressures on villagers to leave the land.[10]

Disinvestment from the countryside and new employment in cities induced new patterns of chain and career migration. Families still expected their children to move in pursuit of jobs, but now older brothers and sisters at work in rapidly growing cities provided an anchor for their younger siblings and cousins. In the late nineteenth century many workers who had immigrated to America still returned to their countries of origin, but not necessarily to their home villages. Some found work in industrial cities, while others, after years abroad, returned to retire.[11]

Jews, of course, were not peasants turned off the land, but as artisans, peddlers, and dealers in local grains, timber, and cattle, they were subject to the same demographic and economic pressures as their clients. The emigration of young male and female farm workers meant that peddlers would have fewer customers, while the railroad brought factory goods that displaced local artisans and peddlers. In Holland, to counter this kind of competition, a few Jewish merchants in small towns used their contacts as peddlers to build a new network to produce cheap cottons. They succeeded partly because Dutch linen manufacturers clung to the idea of cottage industry for local sales as the foundation of family stability. Jewish peddlers, as outsiders with a broader sense of markets, bought cotton waste from a wide array of sources, imported British power looms from relatives in Manchester, and mass-produced cheap cotton cloth for export. They also invested in railroads to create markets for their goods throughout Holland and western Germany.[12]

Most Jewish families lacked the capital to create a new industry, but they turned similar migratory business practices into profitable ends in promising new locales. Several early careers of men later prominent in the American West illustrate how older patterns of migration provided the personal skills that chains of migration turned into new careers.

Harris Newmark, who was born in 1834 in a small village in West Prussia as the sixth child in a growing family, quietly shifted from local and circular migration to chain migration in pursuit of a new career. With the aid of relatives and friends he created a new social and economic niche. His father, Philip, manufactured inks, which he sold as a peddler through the countryside of Sweden. At first Philip was accompanied by his eldest son, J. P. But in 1846 J. P. sought wider opportunities in England and then in New York. By 1851 he had moved on to San Francisco, where he abandoned artisanal crafts and peddling and formed a partnership as a general merchant trading with the gold rush towns. With J. P. departed, Philip in 1849 took fifteen-year-old Harris to Stockholm to teach him the craft of manufacturing inks and the strategies of rural peddling.[13] But the Swedish and Norwegian peasantry continued their rapid emigration from the land, and opportunities for ink peddlers were clearly declining.[14] After four years of seasonal migration, including several trips alone through the Swedish countryside, Harris was sent in 1853 via chain migration to join J. P. In the meantime J. P. had expanded his commercial operations by relocating to the village of Los Angeles, which had become the regional source of farm

Meyer J. and Harris Newmark, c. 1859. In 1853 Harris immigrated to Los Angeles to join his brother as a merchant. From the Archives of *Western States Jewish History*.

produce and beef. Here he became a commodities supplier, buying wheat, vegetables, and cattle, which he shipped to his partner in San Francisco, who resold them to millers and butchers.

Harris's trip from medieval artisan to modern merchant started on 1 July 1853 in Gothenburg, Sweden, and, after a forty-nine-day voyage from Liverpool to New York and a trek a few months later across the Isthmus of Nicaragua, it ended on 21 October, adjacent to the Los Angeles pueblo. The chain included a friend from his village who kept a boardinghouse in New York, a relative in New York who supplied his brief venture as a peddler, his brother's business partner in San Francisco, a gentile commission merchant at the port of San Pedro, and the Jewish treasurer of his brother's Masonic Lodge in Los Angeles, who finally escorted him to J. P.'s store. Distant California had been integrated into the Newmark family migration pattern, but the focus had shifted from circulatory peddling for survival to innovative merchandising for a career. In his lengthy memoirs, Harris recounts somewhat remorsefully, but with no regrets, that he returned to Prussia only twice to see his aging father.[15] Had he any residual need for paternal guidance, he could have received it from his Uncle Joseph, who in 1854 relocated his family to Los Angeles, started a successful general merchandise business, and conducted weekly religious services.[16]

The early experiences of Bernard Goldsmith and his family similarly reflected the shift from circular merchandising to innovative career. Bernard was born in 1832 in a village in Bavaria, where his father was a wool dealer, very dependent on the health of the rural economy. As local pasturage was enclosed for the production of food crops and flax, farm families left for America.[17] When Bernard, the eldest of eight boys, completed gymnasia, he faced the same career choices as did J. P. Newmark. Many years later Goldsmith recalled that "in 1848 [when he was fifteen] there was a general revolution and general dissatisfaction over there and I did not like things and I just made up my mind that I would come here; that was all."[18]

His father, however, hardly thrust him into the unknown. Bernard was sent with several hundred dollars of capital to an uncle in New York, who taught him the rudiments of watchmaking and retail sales. But the gold rush drew him also, and in early 1851, at age nineteen, he landed in San Francisco to join the Jewish mercantile chain. A former employee of his father found him a clerkship in the network of young Jewish merchants. At first Bernard worked in Sacramento for Louis Sloss and then ran pack trains up the Feather River. Fourteen months later a younger brother joined him in San Francisco, and with inventory provided by cousins in New York and Boston, they entered the wholesale jewelry business. Their careers ultimately led them to pack trading and general merchandising in southern Oregon, until they had accumulated enough capital to start a general merchandising business in Portland.

While we assume that few Jews ever returned permanently to Europe, Harris Newmark's memoirs of Los Angeles indicate that, at least prior to 1880, many men retained close contacts and contemplated a circular migration. Many returned to marry, often to sisters of their American business associates. In the 1860s especially, men from Alsace and Bavaria left their brothers in the riskier world of the Pacific Coast and took their profits home. Most, like H. M. Hellman or A. Portugal, had family connections through whom they hoped to restore family fortunes.[19]

The Merchant Niche

Students of the sociology of work have noted that the family networks that sustain ethnic groups generate social capital, or the contacts that enable individuals to coalesce and protect a secure niche in new situations.[20] The young Jewish men helping one another start businesses were creating such a niche so that their families and religious community might acquire a secure social status. While the land was open and the competition only modest, cash was scarce and the physical hardships severe. In an era when people and commodities moved by stagecoach and wagon (until railroads came to Portland, Seattle, and Los Angeles in the 1880s), when bandits murdered peddlers on the roads, and when credit rating services denigrated Jewish business practices as unethical, the risks were substantial. Family interdependence provided a key source of trust.[21]

The oral history of Sylvan Durkheimer, the letters of Ben Selling of Portland, and the memoirs of Harris Newmark provide windows through which to examine the complex economic functions, the dissolving and reknitting of partnerships, and the employment networks linking larger and smaller towns across vast open spaces. Julius Durkheimer, Sylvan's father, had been born in Philadelphia in 1857, the second son in a Bavarian immigrant family that relocated to Portland after the Civil War. His father's mercantile operations shifted from furniture to tobacco and were probably

Left to right: Joseph Newmark, his great-granddaughter Rose Loeb (later Mrs. Henry Levi), his granddaughter Mrs. Leon Loeb (née Estelle Newmark), and his daughter Mrs. Harris Newmark (née Sarah Newmark). From the Archives of *Western States Jewish History.*

never very profitable, because Julius and his brothers were apprenticed with other merchants at printing and bookkeeping.[22] In 1874, at age seventeen, Julius moved almost 300 miles east across the Cascade Range to Baker, Oregon, to clerk for two Jewish general merchants. By 1886 he had saved enough money to open his own store about fifty miles south and west of Baker at Prairie City. He then called his three brothers from Portland to assist him with it and in opening a branch at Canyon City, about thirty miles farther west. By 1889 Julius had sold the Canyon City store to three businessmen and the Prairie City store to his brother Moses and opened a new store at Burns, in southeast Oregon. He felt sufficiently prosperous to marry Delia Fried, the daughter of another Bavarian immigrant who had also settled in Portland, and begin a family.

Durkheimer had located himself and his young family 150 miles from the nearest railroad, among sheep and cattle ranches, and shut off from the outside world by snow for five months of the year. In such an isolated setting, the key to his success lay in his ability to provide credit over the growing season to ranchers who needed supplies but lacked cash. He became a wholesale seller of grain, corn, and even cattle to commission merchants in Portland.[23] Harris Newmark in Los Angeles was virtually forced into the exporting of produce and hides, which he took in exchange for clothing. His brother, who relocated permanently to San Francisco in 1858 as a commission merchant, effectively became his agent and supplier.[24] S. H. Friendly, in Eugene, a town of 1,100 in 1880, was the leading buyer of hops and wheat, commodities he shipped to his brother Charles, a commission merchant in Portland, who no doubt shipped the surplus to colleagues in San Francisco.[25] As William Cronon has noted, "Without the storekeepers' willingness to purchase produce and extend credit in advance of the harvest, many farmers would not have survived their own lack of capital in growing crops and bringing them to market."[26]

Providing supplies and credit for ranchers, defending the town of Burns as a member of the militia, and serving as mayor in 1895, Julius Durkheimer exemplified the frugal and civic-minded merchant. (Likewise, his brother Moses settled into Prairie City, where he served as mayor and operated his store until his accidental death in 1919.) But Julius had promised his wife that within ten years of their marriage he would be able financially to return to Portland to provide better schooling for the children and Jewish companionship for her. By 1897 he had kept his word, selling the store and investing his savings in Portland's largest wholesale grocery company. The family could return to its base, where Delia quickly became an officer in the Ladies Hebrew Benevolent Society.

Where Julius acquired the capital to establish his first store is unclear, although a dozen years of clerking should have provided more than enough time to save. Harris Newmark had earned $1,500 in seven months in 1854 as proprietor of his first store, which he bought from his brother.[27] Ben Selling, in his many letters to friends and business partners, illustrated how young men should be able to make a living in a country store and how a wholesale merchant could profit from sustaining the network. Selling assumed that managers of country stores needed training as clerks, but with good supply connections and a shrewd assessment of the farmers who had to be carried on credit, they should be able to earn between $2,000 to $3,000 a year. While country storekeepers had to extend credit, Selling constantly admonished his partner, Gus Winckler, at a general store in Bend for extending credit from season to season instead of trying to acquire cash. When Winckler wrote that he held cattle that could be sold for $4,000, Selling insisted the sale be made and the cash forwarded to pay off suppliers and to use as collateral for resupply.[28]

Selling tried to develop as much control over the supply and sales chains as possible by eliminating competition from San Francisco merchants. He bought almost exclusively from Jewish supply houses in Portland, like Flieschner-Mayer for dry goods, Neustadter for boots and shoes, and M. Seller for crockery. He even invested in an underwear factory in Portland so he could cut costs by keeping San Francisco suppliers out of the market. His Portland operations remained in family hands. He served as commission merchant for an uncle who owned a store in Pendleton and for a friend who had one in Prineville. One brother served as Selling's collector in country districts; another, as his bookkeeper. He contemplated sending a third, whom he often criticized for lacking the self-discipline to run a country store, to Chicago, where the bright lights might keep him interested while he served as a buyer in the new garment industry.[29]

Jewish merchants in San Francisco in the 1850s, starting with less capital than native-born tradesmen, generally succeeded by avoiding risky speculation.[30] Selling seems to have learned this lesson from his father and passed it on to younger men asking his advice. While he might occasionally show interest in investing in short-term ventures, like land for raising sheep or for harvesting timber, or a single venture, like importing bulk coffee, he avoided mining stocks or investments that might tie up capital. Despite the family's substantial wealth, he persisted in shrewd business practices to sustain his mercantile network. When Selling sold his general store in Prineville to Leo Senders and Moses Sternberg of Albany in 1883, he instructed his resident manager to quietly rent a store nearby so he might sell off the inventory rather than returning it to Portland. When the rented building burned down a few months later, he was able to get a friend appointed as appraiser and collected the full insurance value for his stock.[31]

The stories of Durkheimer and Selling suggest that although they controlled a small network of general stores, they had substantial Jewish competition. Harriet Levy observed that while her father and his colleagues did compete for business, many lessened the direct competition by developing specialties in different commodities and by helping one another though benevolent societies. The minutes of several such organizations indicate that they accumulated capital to lend to members at below prevailing interest rates. Individuals like Benish Levy or Philip Selling were able to retire in their late fifties or early sixties because they lent capital at interest to their younger colleagues. They based their assessment of worthiness not on credit ratings but on their personal knowledge of the younger men's characters.[32]

The Social
Network and the
New Life Cycle

The relationships between Jewish merchants illustrate how towns of varying sizes performed different functions and how families kept contacts open to assist one another. For example, San Francisco, as the regional manufacturing center, held a unique clothing factory, that of Levi Strauss, and paper box factories, like those of the Zellerbachs and the Fleishackers. As the region's importing emporium, it was also headquarters for Sloss and Gerstle's Alaska Commercial Company, which held a franchise for hunting fur seals and also owned fish canneries, and for the Brandenstein brothers' wholesale importing house.[33] In the Pacific Northwest, Portland had the biggest market for goods and services. Consequently, it had the largest number of merchants specializing in the supply of specific finished products (like crockery, liquors, and cigars), the largest amount of artisans, and the largest proportion of clerks, who were being trained to manage stores. Jeanette Hirsch Meier, for example, brought several of her brothers from their village, Worms-am-Rhine, to work in the family's growing general merchandise business. The Fleishner, Mayer, and Solomon Hirsch families organized the Pacific Northwest's largest wholesale dry goods house, which employed many sons and nephews as clerks and traveling agents.[34] Los Angeles, on the cusp of a speculative land boom, was close behind Portland in the proportion of young clerks and in the array of tailors and other artisans. The Newmarks encouraged young men from their village of Loebau to emigrate, and the Jacoby, Cohn, and Lewin brothers all came, as did the Hellmans, Haases, and Fleischmans from Rechendsdorf, Bavaria.[35]

Towns of 10,000 to 20,000 residents along the Pacific Coast, like Los Angeles and Portland, attracted groups of Jewish brothers and cousins from all over Central Europe, including Alsace, Bavaria, Prussia, Baden, and Wurtemburg, and smaller numbers from Bohemia, Austria, Switzerland, and England. Even Albany, Oregon, the tiny commercial hub of the southern Willamette Valley, with 1,800 people and only 25 Jewish adult males in 1880, drew them from Alsace, Bavaria, Prussia, Poland, Austria, and Hungary (see table 4). The boomtown of Virginia City, Nevada, in the 1870s attracted a few Alsatians, Bavarians, and Austrians, but primarily newcomers from Prussia, Posen, and Russia.

The various categories of employment usually coincided with a stage in the male life cycle (see tables 2 and 3). Almost 90 percent of the clerks were age thirty or younger, while almost as high a proportion of merchants were over age thirty. Men in their early thirties were ready to act as traveling agents in liquors, hides, furs, even sugar, and might spend part of the year in the country districts and the rest in a larger mercantile center. The handful of young men residing in rooming houses, rather than in the homes of

Town	Total Population	Jewish Population Number	% Jewish	Percent Jews 0-16 years old
Portland, OR	17,577	508	2.9	43.9
Albany, OR	1,867	72	3.9	36.1
Seattle, WA Terr.	3,533	98	2.8	48.0
Los Angeles, CA	11,183	420	3.8	48.3
Virginia City, NV	10,917	146	1.3	46.6
Carson City, NV	4,229	86	2.0	57.0
Reno, NV	1,302	75	5.8	38.7
Trinidad, CO*	5,345	170	3.2	31.2

*1900 data

Table 1: Jewish Population, Selected Western Towns, 1880

Occupation	Portland	Seattle	Los Angeles	Nevada towns*	Number	Percent
Merchant	65	11	49	36	161	41.6
Capitalist	7	0	3	5	15	3.9
Jeweler	2	2	2	3	9	2.3
Clerk/agent	50	6	27	21	104	26.9
Peddler/grocer	3	0	1	0	4	1.0
Saloon	3	3	4	2	12	3.1
Rabbi/teacher	2	1	1	0	4	1.0
Other professional	4	1	4	0	9	2.3
Tailor	11	2	5	9	27	7.0
Other artisan	11	6	8	0	25	6.5
Service	4	4	3	2	13	3.4
Laborer	1	1	2	0	4	1.0
Total	163	37	109	78	387	100.0

*Virginia City, Carson City, Reno

Table 2: Jewish Male Employment, Selected Western Towns, 1880

City	Number of Jews	No. Jews Male	% males 0-16	% males 17-30	% males 31-50	% males 51+
Portland, OR	508	279	40.9	22.2	30.5	6.5
Albany, OR	72	38	31.6	21.0	39.5	7.9
Seattle, WA Terr.	98	53	43.4	16.9	32.1	9.4
Los Angeles, CA	420	224	45.1	23.7	23.3	8.0
Virginia City, NV	146	72	41.7	13.8	31.9	12.5
Carson City, NV	86	42	50.0	14.3	28.5	7.1
Reno, NV	75	41	39.0	21.9	29.3	9.8

Table 3: Jewish Male Age Profile, Selected Western Towns, 1880

merchants, in cities like Los Angeles, Portland, and even Virginia City and Albany, were usually traveling agents. Craftsmen like tailors, printers, cigar makers, and barbers ranged more evenly by age over the life cycle. The young barbers and tailors were often working for older shop proprietors.

Young men, of course, depended on a network of relatives to find mercantile apprenticeships, and family settlement patterns largely met these needs. The small community of Albany, with only twenty-six employed Jewish men, nicely illustrates how social connections reinforced the employment network. The Cohen brothers from Posen, for example, found places in their households for men named Salinger. Aaron Cohen's father-in-law, L. Salinger, a retired merchant in his mid-seventies, lived with him, his wife, and five young children, while Samuel Cohen housed and employed Otto Salinger, age twenty-five, as a cigar maker and clerk. I. J. Jackson, a merchant from Poland, employed Nathan Kalisky, his new son-in-law, as his clerk. Moses Sternberg, the grain dealer, found a place in his household for his nephew, Sol Mannheim, whom he also employed as a clerk.[36]

Family connections reached beyond tiny Albany to larger fields for training and employment. Julius and Elvira Gradwohl, a couple in their mid-forties who ran a general store and combined Alsatian and Prussian family connections, more than likely arranged for twenty-one-year-old Maurice Gradwohl to clerk for the Los Angeles merchant Adolph Cohn. Adolph was in turn related to Isadore, Bernard, and Kaspare Cohn, who were related to the Cohn merchants of Virginia City as well as to Harris Newmark and his clan of brothers scattered between San Francisco and Los Angeles.[37]

The distribution of adults by age cohort and the ratio of men to women in different towns illustrate how men and women migrated during their life cycles. As late as 1880, men outnumbered women everywhere, as young men, many born on the East Coast or in California, were clerking in the larger towns or helping to manage stores in small ones. But the long-

Place of Birth	Portland	Albany OR	Seattle	Los Angeles	Virginia City	Carson City	Reno	Total No.	% of Total
France/Alsace	4	5	1	11	2	1	2	26	5.7
Bavaria	26	4	6	13	4	0	1	54	12.4
Prussia	54	8	9	37	17	16	12	153	35.2
Baden, etc.	9	0	2	4	1	2	2	20	4.6
"Germany"	17	0	3	14	0	0	0	34	7.8
Aust-Hung	2	6	1	1	3	0	0	13	3.0
Other	12	3	1	17	10	1	2	46	10.6
USA									
East Coast	16	1	3	10	1	1	2	34	7.8
Midwest	1	0	0	3	1	0	0	5	1.1
Oregon	9	1	0	0	0	0	0	10	2.3
California	14	0	1	15	2	1	2	35	8.0
Other West	0	0	1	0	2	0	0	3	0.7
Canada	0	0	1	0	0	0	1	2	0.5
Total	164	28	29	125	43	22	24	435	100.0

Table 4: Place of Birth, Jewish Adult Males, Selected Western Towns, 1880

term goal of most Jewish men was to establish a family, and very few Jewish men beyond their mid-thirties were unmarried. Therefore, in many smaller towns, women between seventeen and thirty often outnumbered men, because as young men moved to larger towns as clerks, young women would be marrying and moving to small towns as the wives of merchants (see table 5).

Harriet Levy in San Francisco captured this transit very well when she noted that if a girl were not married young to a local man, she would be fated for an older bachelor from an interior town. "Shopkeepers came to the city from the interior, from the towns of the San Joaquin or Sacramento valleys, or from the mining towns . . . to buy goods. Their quest often included a sentimental hope, confided to a downtown wholesale merchant. If a man's appearance was agreeable and his credit good, he would be invited to the merchant's home to dine and meet the unmarried daughters."[38]

The accuracy of Levy's uncharitable observation is supported by census data. In Virginia City and Reno as well as in the much larger community of Los Angeles, all within the social purview of San Francisco, over 60 percent of the married men had wives at least eight years younger than themselves. And in Portland, 54 percent of the men were at least eight years older than their wives, with another 28 percent from four to seven years older (see table 6). In such marriages, men who were already established in their careers as supervisors of stores, employers of clerks, and often with civic status in Masonic and B'nai B'rith lodges, tried also to impose control over the household. As Alice Gerstle Levison, a daughter of the wealthy co-owner of the Alaska Commercial Company, recalled, her father was fifteen years older than her mother, whom he treated "like a little girl who had to be protected."[39]

Merchants in the interior might not have to venture so far to find a wife. Philip Lewis of Ellensburg, Washington, somehow met Bella Senders, the oldest daughter of Leo Senders of Albany, Oregon, and brought her home as his bride in the 1880s. When Bella's younger sister Amelia visited Ellensburg, she met a young immigrant named Henry Kleinberg, whom she soon married. Kleinberg, though trained as a tailor in Posen, became a hay and grain merchant like his father-in-law and bought land on the outskirts

Town	Adult Males			Adult Females		
	17-30 yrs	31-51+yrs	Total	17-30 yrs	31-51+yrs	Total
Portland	62	103	165	67	53	120
Albany	8	18	26	8	7	17
Seattle	9	21	30	7	14	21
Los Angeles	53	70	123	55	41	96
Virginia City	10	32	42	20	16	36
Carson City	6	15	21	8	8	16

Table 5: Population Breakdown by Gender and Age, Selected Western Jewish Communities, 1880

	Wife older	Husband 0-3 years older	Husband 4-7 years older	Husband 8-12 years older	Husband 12+ years older	Total
Albany	0	2	8	3	2	15
Seattle	2	4	5	2	5	18
Virginia City	0	6	7	6	13	32
Carson City	0	4	4	3	3	14
Reno	1	0	2	4	8	15
Los Angeles	3	12	10	21	17	63

Table 6: Age of Husband Relative to Age of Wife, Jews in Selected Western Towns, 1880

Number of children present	Households with married couples or widows present						
	Portland	Seattle	Albany	Los Angeles	Virginia City	Carson City	Reno
0	12	1	4	7	3	0	2
1	15	3	3	6	6	1	3
2	13	5	2	14	3	4	3
3	8	3	2	13	6	4	2
4	17	0	1	12	7	0	2
5	9	3	2	4	3	2	1
6	8	1	1	7	1	1	1
7	3	1	0	3	0	2	0
8	0	0	0	2	0	0	0
9	0	0	0	2	0	0	0
Households	85	17	15	70	29	14	14

Table 7: Children Present in Jewish Households, Selected Western Towns, 1880

of Ellensburg that he rented to farmers. But while Leo Senders and his sons remained in their small town as commission merchants, Bella and Amelia pressured their husbands to move to Seattle to raise their families in a Jewish communal setting. According to his daughter, however, Kleinberg, like his father-in-law, like the Sanders and Jaffas of Trinidad, Colorado, like the Spiegelbergs of Santa Fe, or like Seymour Friendly of Eugene, preferred living as a respected commission merchant and landowner in a small town. He had enjoyed the friendly greetings that a merchant received daily on the streets of the town, where he had contributed to the YMCA and helped finance the streetlights. "In Ellensburg everybody called him Henry. On the street they'd say, 'Hi, Henry.' He never liked the formality of a larger city. He adjusted, of course," his daughter reassured her interviewer.[40]

Nevertheless, the daring migration of young men from Central Europe to help create a new market system in the western United States seems to have been balanced by the desire to create in their personal lives traditional patriarchal patterns. The loss of contact with the family of origin seems to have led many men to replicate at least some of its patterns in the households they were creating. The disparity in age between husband and wife was probably greater than that of their parents in Central Europe. But when a man married, usually in his mid-thirties, he and his wife had children almost immediately. In 1880, children under age sixteen were about 45 percent of the Jewish population everywhere, and this pattern emerged in towns where about 20 percent of the Jewish men were young unmarried clerks. For our sample of towns, if we examine the 88 percent of the households for which at least one child was present, the median number of children in the household was three or four (see table 7). The larger towns, Portland and Los Angeles, had the great bulk of the older, wealthier, and larger households and the higher number of children per household. At a time when native-born, white, urban, middle-class families had fewer and fewer children,[41] the households of immigrant Jewish merchants might include six or more. In addition, the census data reflects only those children present, not those who had moved out to clerk or to marry. While many Jewish mercantile households had servants, primarily Irish women and occasionally, in a very wealthy household, a Chinese man, the wives of immigrant merchants were kept busy caring for children.

Available data also undercounts the number of children ever born and consequently does not reflect the continual tragedy of infant and childhood mortality. Many larger families with most children born a year or two apart had gaps of several years between some of them. The record of deaths kept by the rabbis at Temple Beth Israel in Portland in the late nineteenth century shows that between 1877 and 1885 slightly more than half of seventy-seven deaths were of children under age seventeen, and the great majority of these were below the age of nine years.[42] Harris Newmark, amidst the voluminous details of his business career and those of his friends, provides a personal view of how tragedy might strike. He and his wife had nine children, only four of whom survived to adulthood. One died at age one month in the early 1860s, a daughter died at age six in 1874, while in 1879 three sons, ages nine, five, and three, died within a few weeks of each other from diphtheria.[43]

The households also reflected several other patterns that reinforced a patriarchal tradition. Unmarried daughters, of course, remained at home and almost never worked prior to marriage. But unmarried sons resided at home also, unless they were sent as clerks to small towns. While a few unmarried Jewish clerks did live in boardinghouses, even in small towns like Carson City or Albany, most lived with their employer. Prosperous households like those of Maurice Kremer, Samuel Norton, Samuel Prager, and Samuel Meyers of Los Angeles; Bernard Goldsmith, Solomon Hirsch, Mathias Koshland, Aaron Meier, and Harry Wolf of Portland; S. Michaelson of Virginia City; and Moses Sternberg and I. J. Jackson of Albany included elderly in-laws and unmarried sisters-in-law, nephews, clerks, and servants. Kremer's household, in addition to his wife and six children, held his elderly cousin, Joseph Newmark; Newmark's son, Morris; and his nephew, Marx Cohn; as well as two servants. Goldsmith's household held, in addition to his wife and six children, two nephews who were clerks and two servants. Meier's household, in addition to his wife and three children, held his younger partner, Sigmund Frank, and his wife's two brothers, who were clerks in his general store.[44]

In addition, married children occasionally remained in their parents' household or, more frequently, moved between it and their own home as family circumstances required. When Ben Selling's retired parents went to Germany for a prolonged vacation, he rented his own house and moved his family back to his parent's larger home. He, his wife, and their children remained there for many years, even after his parents returned. Although elderly parents seldom emigrated from Germany to retire with their children, as the immigrant generation aged, widows and widowers expected to move in with their children. And, as Harriet Levy noted, nephews and nieces might arrive with little warning from relatives in Germany who expected that places could be found or matches made for them in the limitless American wilderness.[45]

Temple Block, downtown Los Angeles, c. 1880s, showing the Jacoby Brothers store. From the photo collection of the Los Angeles Public Library.

The Jewish Public Presence

Jewish merchants created communities by renting contiguous stores on the main business blocks, sending their sons for mercantile apprenticeships to relatives or friends, and marrying their daughters to other established merchants. By examining profiles of a number of selected towns in Oregon, Nevada, California, and Washington in 1880, we can appreciate how Jewish merchants constructed communities, passed on skills, and prepared their children to succeed as the West became more economically integrated and sophisticated. If a change in migration patterns enabled young men from the 1850s through the 1870s to innovate in a region badly in need of supplies, credit, and investment, the introduction of more sophisticated methods of transportation and sales required that their sons continue to accumulate contacts and capital and even to adjust their family structure to modern cities.

The towns of Seattle, Tacoma, Portland, Albany, Los Angeles, Virginia City, Carson City, and Reno were part of a regional marketing network focused on San Francisco. Taking a commuter train today from Eugene to Seattle would take one within a few blocks of the former locations of the interlocking network of Jewish merchants. The railroad depot in Eugene at the head of Willamette Street was three blocks north of a half dozen stores, including those of S. H. Friendly, dry goods; Abe Goldsmith, cigars; and Aaron Goldsmith, groceries and crockery. Sixty miles north, along First Street in Albany, Jews presented a more intensive mercantile image by occupying fourteen stores stretching for two blocks along either side of First Street, the main business thoroughfare. They occupied four more around the corner on Second Street.[46] At Portland the railroad passes along the eastern shore of the Willamette River, which it crosses just north of the main business district, where Jewish wholesale supply houses were situated.

The Washington towns of Longview, Centralia, Chehalis, and Olympia each had a few Jewish merchants, but most were located along Puget Sound. When the Northern Pacific reached Tacoma, it passed a block west of the general stores of Meyer Kaufman and Louis Wolff at Second and McCarver Streets in Old Town. As it curved east from the sound toward the new downtown, it passed a block west of Pacific Avenue, where between Eleventh and Sixteenth Streets were located David Levin's barber shop, Abraham Gross's dry goods store, the general store of Adolph Pachscher, and both the general store and grocery store maintained by R. J. Weisbach. When it reached its terminal about forty miles north at Second and Jackson Streets in downtown Seattle, passengers were within two blocks of H. Auerbach, dry goods, and P. Singerman, general merchant on Commercial Street. But in this remote corner of Washington, Jews were fewer and their stores far less clustered than in the Oregon towns. There were, however, eight Jewish businesses near Second and Marion Streets, within five blocks of the terminal, including Joseph Goldstein, who was speculating as a "capitalist," and Joseph Isaacs, who had an auction yard at Front and Marion.[47]

Los Angeles before the real estate boom of the mid-1880s held a very different population than the cities of the Pacific Northwest, northern California, and Nevada. Not only its climate but also its people could be described as Mediterranean. Many railroad workers, ranch hands, day laborers, and artisans, like saddlers and blacksmiths, came from Mexico or were Californians of Mexican descent. Some of the professionals and landholders had been born in Spain. Storekeepers and many of the artisans had emigrated from France and Italy as well as from the various German

Los Angeles, California, c. 1875. Visible are the stores of Harris and Jacoby (formerly I. W. Hellman), Maurice Kremer, and Solomon Lazard. From the Archives of *Western States Jewish History.*

states; the French Benevolent Society was the town's oldest and largest. The Jewish merchants of Alsace, Bavaria, and Prussia blended easily into the cosmopolitan cultural mix. Jews served for decades as French consuls, and Harris Newmark spoke Spanish before he learned English.[48]

The first Los Angeles city directory in 1872 carried advertisements from a dozen Jewish storekeepers, as well as I. W. Hellman and John Downey's Farmers & Merchants Bank. The stores were clustered within two or three blocks of each other, along Commercial Street, which ran east and west, and its intersections with Los Angeles and Main Streets, both of which ran north and south. Sam Prager, dealer in dry goods, boots, and shoes, was on one corner of Commercial and Los Angeles Streets, while S. Goldstein's "The White House" was on another. At number 3 Commercial was S. Nordlinger, watches, clocks, and jewelry, and at number 7 was Sam Meyer, retail crockery and glassware. A block to the west along Main Street at number 51 was S. Lazard, wholesale dry goods; at number 63, Harris and Jacoby, gents furnishings, books, stationery, and cigars; at number 95, S. Hellman, books, stationery, and cigars; and at number 97, J. Strelitz, merchant tailor. Harris Newmark, who sold groceries, liquors, and provisions in exchange for hides and grains, was nearby at numbers 5 and 6, Arcadia block, near Lips and des Autels, wholesale liquors, corner of Main and Arcadia.[49]

Arriving in Virginia City in 1880 at the railroad depot at D and Union Streets, a passenger would walk a block or two uphill along Union and past the Frederick House and the International Hotel to reach the commercial district that stretched two blocks north and south of Union along A, B, and C Streets. Here he would find Jews running saloons, barbershops, tailoring establishments, tobacco stores, and numerous clothing emporiums as well as Celia Goldman's lodging house at 102 North C Street. As in Albany and Los Angeles, so in Virginia City the "Jew next door" presented himself intensively as the Main Street merchant.[50] Whatever mythic images of the Jew the miners, farmers, and others may have brought west with them, a brief walk from the train station in dozens of towns and a perusal of city directories listing officers of Masonic lodges and members of city councils and school boards would have substituted the impression of civic booster. Harriet Levy captured a "citified" glimpse of the merchant in the country town when she described Jacob Meyer, who came to her sister's wedding from Virginia City. Levy describes the man, then in his mid-fifties, as having long legs, glossy black hair, and slim beard. "He looked like a gambler from Poker Flats," she wrote, no doubt a romantic and flattering description of a man who, with his wife and daughter, ran a millinery business next door to his brother's tailor shop on North A Street.[51]

The Civic Veneer: Benevolence and the Spoils of Office

Young merchants on the move had to be concerned with their health and with minimal ritual requirements, and the network of brothers and cousins created institutions and a public persona to provide collective security. As early as 1856 Henry Labbatt, a Jewish lawyer in San Francisco, responded to accusations that Jews were unwilling to create a permanent stake in the land by pointing to the brick synagogues, which symbolized commitment to local communities, and to the benevolent societies, which relieved the state of welfare costs.[52] Hebrew benevolent societies and cemetery associations appeared everywhere to pay for medical care and to bury the victims of disease, accidents, and violence. The primary rituals men conducted, in addition to burial, were annual high holiday services, initially observed in rented rooms. But as men married and started families, they organized their religious obligations through formally incorporated synagogues. I. J. Benjamin, traveling through northern California in 1860, found young Jewish merchants who had already organized benevolent societies and synagogues at Sacramento, Stockton, Marysville, Placerville, Nevada City, Grass Valley, and Folsom.[53]

The synagogue became the architectural expression of the Jewish community's status as a pillar of the new society. San Francisco's magnificent Temple Emanu-El, with its twin spires topped by bronze-plated domes resembling the rimmonim on the sefer Torah, expressed Jewish leadership in the regional metropolis. Located on Sutter Street, it remained a downtown landmark until the earthquake in 1906.[54] Portland's Beth Israel commissioned a smaller but similarly elaborate twin-towered brick struc-

Jaffa Mercantile Company,
Trinidad, Colorado, c. 1870.

ture in 1889.[55] The 1892 Trinidad, Colorado, city directory featured an etching of the Jewish synagogue, Congregation Aaron, which was erected of brick and stone in 1889 and located two blocks down Maples Street from the courthouse. It made the single-spired Methodist Church featured on the opposite page seem parsimonious by comparison.[56]

While rabbis might complain about sparse attendance at Sabbath observances, Jewish merchants and clerks entered energetically into the secular fellowship of Jewish fraternalism and non-denominational Masonry. As Hasia R. Diner has demonstrated, "No organization captured the character of nineteenth-century American Jewish communal culture as clearly as B'nai B'rith."[57] In San Francisco in 1855 about a dozen young men petitioned the New York headquarters of the B'nai B'rith for a charter, and by November they had organized the first lodge on the Pacific Coast, Ophir Lodge No. 21. By 1863 there were eight lodges on the Pacific Coast, and Grand District Lodge No. 4 was installed in San Francisco to create a regional focus for conventions and an actuarial pool to support the insurance benefits.[58] The intensity of a network sustaining a lodge can be seen as late as 1897 by examining the employment and residential points of contact among the eleven men who were then the officers of Seattle's Lodge No. 342. Three, Maurice Greenbaum, Kassell Gottstein, and Louis Schoenfeld, owned large businesses in downtown Seattle. They were patriarchs of families in which several sons, employed as their clerks, also lived in their homes. Two other officers clerked for Schwabacher Brothers, and four others clerked for other Jewish businesses. Eight lived either next door to or across the street from a fellow officer in a new residential area overlooking the downtown near Thirteenth Street and Yesler Way.[59]

The lodges at first collected dues to cover health and death benefits for the members, and meetings were devoted to the discussion of the welfare of individuals and to male entertainment at cards and billiards. By the late 1880s lodges increased in number, partly because of the spread of the Jewish mercantile network to cities like Seattle and Virginia City and also because younger clerks wished to establish a new actuarial pool so that

Etching of the Jewish synagogue Congregation Aaron, erected of brick and stone in 1889, from the Trinidad, Colorado, city directory of 1892. Courtesy of the Colorado Historical Society, Denver.

their dues would not be paid out as benefits to men of their fathers' generation. Indeed, by the late 1890s, life insurance in larger amounts would be made available by national companies that employed local Jewish agents, making the B'nai B'rith benefit obsolete.

In addition, the greater affluence of Jewish families by the 1880s led the Grand District Lodge to see a broader scope for charity, while many members used local lodge meetings to express their genteel civic status. The Grand District Lodge responded to a mounting social problem by starting a regional Jewish orphanage in San Francisco and taxing local lodges for its support. At the local level, lodge meetings of the younger men, many of whom had been raised in Portland or San Francisco, shifted their focus from exclusive male fellowship to elegant entertainment and socializing with female guests. By the 1890s, Portland Lodge No. 416, whose members included many sons of wealthy merchant families, had as its social chairman Samuel Friedlander, manager of the city's exclusive Marquam Opera House. He organized lodge programs featuring vocal and instrumental solos by the wives and female friends of members. Card playing and dancing usually followed.[60]

Many Jewish merchants and clerks not only attended their B'nai B'rith lodge meetings twice a month, they were also drawn into the world of Masonry. City directories in towns like Los Angeles, Portland, Seattle, Spokane, and San Francisco list dozens of lodges of Odd Fellows, Red Men, Wood Men, as well as Masons, not to mention the Eastern Star and the Ancient Order of Hibernians. The core of town socializing was enacted at the twice-monthly meetings of these lodges and benevolent clubs. Men who could pay dues to a B'nai B'rith lodge, a Masonic lodge, and some other social club would have a place to congregate with male companions at least six evenings each month. Jewish merchants became prominent members of the Masons, whose mysterious teachings and emblem glorified

Solomon and the physical builders and spiritual supporters of his temple. Masonic lodges, like the B'nai B'rith, were self-selecting, and Jews usually joined a lodge with gentiles of the same social class, generally fellow merchants and professionals. Jews, who constituted 12 percent of San Francisco's Masonic lodges in the late nineteenth century, were attracted by the spiritual aura attached to the ideology of universal brotherhood and by the civic acceptance that membership conferred.[61] Samuel Meyer of Los Angeles was treasurer of his Masonic lodge for fifty years and brought relatives like the Newmarks with him. Adolph Wolfe, partner in Lipman-Wolfe, Portland's largest department store in the 1890s, took great pride in his status as a lodge officer, and David Solis Cohen was equally proud of his position as Grand Orator of the regional Grand Masonic Lodge, headquartered in San Francisco.[62]

The most conspicuous expression of civic status came through election to public office as members of city councils, mayors, and even members of state legislatures. Small businessmen, who continued to dominate production and sales into the early twentieth century, also dominated office holding in small towns in the Midwest, South, and West.[63] Jewish merchants reinforced this cultural trend. They held all of these offices in many western towns, from a crossroads like Heppner, named for an early Jewish pioneer, to Prescott, Arizona, where Morris Goldwater organized the local bank, financed the railroad to Phoenix, and served as mayor for twenty-two years.[64]

Perhaps the most tightly knit group of Jewish politicians emerged from the merchant clique in Portland, where Joseph Simon, son of a retired merchant, became the state Republican boss in the early 1880s. Trained in the office of the railroad lawyer C. A. Dolph, who was elected for many terms as Portland's mayor and served as Oregon's United States senator, Simon began his political career in 1875 while in his mid-twenties as secretary of the Multnomah County Republican Convention. Twenty years later the legislature chose him as a United States senator. However, he disliked Washington and so returned after one term. In 1910 he was elected mayor of Portland. His circle included Ben Selling, who served several terms in the Oregon state senate; Solomon Hirsch, who served as United States ambassador to the Ottoman Empire under President Benjamin Harrison; and Hirsch's nephew, Sig Sichel, who was elected to the Oregon legislature.[65]

The most colorful image of Jewish civic leadership came in the Southwest, where in the 1880s the mercurial Solomon Bibo (see p. 8) married an Acoma woman and became governor of the pueblo. But photos of him reveal a man equally tied to a mercantile network, because he was

Joseph Simon, Oregon State legislator (1880–92), U. S. senator (1898–1903), and mayor of Portland (1910–11). Photo courtesy of the Oregon Jewish Museum, Portland.

accompanied by younger colleagues who assisted him in his work as the pueblo's supply agent. Bibo, a Prussian emigrant, like Newmark, had come to the United States in 1869 at age sixteen to join two older brothers who had established a general merchandising business in Santa Fe. He developed a special interest in the struggle of the Acoma to regain land, and he learned enough of their language and of American law to assist the tribe in its court case. By the 1890s, however, he and his wife had relocated to San Francisco, where he carried on a mercantile career.[66]

Perhaps more representative was Charles Strauss, the mayor of Tucson in the 1880s. An extraordinary photograph (see p. 106) shows him as a narrow-shouldered man looking soberly at the camera. In his left hand he holds the double barrel of a rifle, with its butt resting on the floor; a cigar dangles between the index and middle finger of his right hand. He wears a gun belt studded with bullets around his waist. A youngster, most likely his son, stands at his side similarly armed. This immigrant from a Bavarian village initiated the building of Tucson's city hall, fire station, and library and created its first building and loan association. Had he moved to Munich or remained in New York, he would never have been addressed as Mr. Mayor nor wielded the militant artifacts of civic power. Nor could he have passed on to his offspring the self-assurance and sense of authority that came from creating the economic and social ties through which so many new towns of the West were knit together.

Epilogue to the Frontier: Jewish Merchants in an Age of Class Tensions

From the late 1890s through World War I, the societies in which Jewish merchants had operated changed their relationship to the larger American economy, thereby affecting both the scale of merchandising and the civic status of Jews. As western cities like Los Angeles, Portland, Seattle, and San Francisco grew rapidly to 250,000 or more, they also became more economically stratified, resembling more closely the midsized cities of the East and Midwest, like Cleveland, Indianapolis, or Milwaukee. Jewish communities, like the population of the cities as a whole, became sharply divided along ethnic and class lines, while the image of Jews became divided as well. The older wholesale supply houses, typified by Schwabacher, the Alaska Commercial Company, and Labatt Freres in San Francisco; Flieschner-Mayer in Portland; Harris Newmark in Los Angeles; or the Gottsteins in Seattle, were superceded in public visibility (and probably in capitalization) by the innovative merchandising phenomenon of the new age of mass consumption, the department store.[67] Pioneer Jewish families like the Hamburgers, Meiers, Lipmans, Magnins, and Goldwaters, who were not always at first the most successful, owned many of the most prominent department stores, but they faced significant gentile competition. In Spokane, the largest retail store was the Palace Department Store, run by the Weil family, but four other department stores run by non-Jews were also listed in the city directory. In Los Angeles, Broadway Department Store and Hamburger & Sons were Jewish, but at least three others were not.

As mines became less productive and miners left, so did the storekeepers, Jews as well as gentiles. But many of the Jewish merchants in small farming towns, like Julius Durkheimer and Philip Lewis, were pushed by their wives to sell their businesses and return to the larger cities, where their children would have access to a Jewish community for social as well as educational reasons. The Jewish merchant enclaves in Albany and Trinidad withered away, leaving a cemetery and synagogue, respectively. Some merchants, like Isaac Lipman and Moses Hamburger, left Nevada towns, found partners in Portland or Los Angeles, and created major department stores. Others, such as Julius Durkheimer, bought into established wholesale houses in cities like Portland, while Bernard Goldsmith's sons, leaving retailing for professional careers, moved from Portland to more rapidly growing Seattle. Ben Selling's only son became a doctor and was not interested in entering the family business, which closed in the mid-1920s. In more isolated New Mexico, the Ilfelds and Spiegelbergs moved from stagnant towns like Santa Fe and Las Vegas to the growing center of Albuquerque.[68]

At the other end of the social spectrum, the largest western cities for the first time developed new and distinctive immigrant neighborhoods. In Denver, Portland, Seattle, and Los Angeles, eastern European Jews shared these predominantly residential areas on the fringes of the central business district with Italian, Serb, or Japanese families. Here appeared a Jewish merchant new to the West but familiar in Warsaw, Vilna, and the towns of southeast Europe: the small retailer selling either exclusively to his fellow Jews or to the working class. Some merchants had small retail shops along the neighborhood's main business street and specialized in foods like meat, fish, baked goods, and other commodities for Jews and their immigrant neighbors. Others had stores adjacent to the waterfront in Seattle and Portland or the railroad yards in Los Angeles, Denver, and San Francisco that sold secondhand goods like clothing or furniture to an ethnically

Charles Strauss and son. Strauss was elected mayor of Tucson in 1883. Courtesy of the Arizona Historical Society, Tucson.

diverse working class. Still others gathered scrap metal and "junk" that was sold to local foundries. Whether located in their residential neighborhoods or near the waterfront, immigrant Jewish storekeepers did not expect to form partnerships or to socialize with gentiles. They did not seek admission to predominantly gentile Masonic lodges, but instead found camaraderie in new B'nai B'rith and B'nai Abraham lodges as well as through smaller neighborhood benevolent societies and proto-Zionist organizations. Seattle and Portland even had their own exotic Jewish immigrant subcommunity, Sephardim from Rhodes and Istanbul. Their small retailers at first specialized in bootblack stands, fish markets, and groceries, where they employed their sons and cousins.[69]

In such dramatically changing cities, with high-rise construction constantly obliterating old landscapes, the old Main Street quickly faded into an unfashionable row of dingy, overcrowded stores.[70] Ben Selling's expanded Eastern Outfitting Company in Portland, or L. H. Guldman's Golden Eagle Dry Goods in Denver, with their low prices and cluttered display windows in large, three-story buildings, were old-fashioned[71] when compared to the cultivated elegance of I. Magnin's in San Francisco, Meier & Frank in Portland, and A. Hamburger & Sons in Los Angeles. All of these department stores had growing lines of merchandise and new, taller structures emulating Philadelphia's John Wanamaker's or New York's B. Altman, Lord & Taylor, or Macy's.[72] Baron Goldwater in Phoenix saw his store as an elite emporium selling only the finest imported items. In Portland, Jeannette Meier, the power behind the city's most prominent high-rise retail icon at Fifth and Morrison, sent several of her nephews as "apprentices" to Wanamaker's, from which they brought to the

West Coast modern concepts of sales, display, and newspaper advertising.[73] In Los Angeles in 1906, Hamburger's new store, occupying almost an entire block, made South Broadway at Eighth a major shopping intersection. In San Francisco after the earthquake, I. Magnin & Company and Raphael Weil & Company located not along the hastily rebuilt Market Street, but on the more fashionable Grant Street near the intersection with Geary and within a block of Union Square.[74] The acquisition of a new cosmopolitan image and distinctive architecture was reinforced by a modernized corporate structure. Entries for department stores in city directories no longer listed "proprietors" but "officers," usually a president, vice-president, secretary-treasurer, and manager.[75]

Likewise, the image of the Jewish merchant as a pillar of civic stability faded into an idyllic past. In cities now socially stratified and geographically segmented by class and race, the new image of the Jew was as dramatically divided as the city itself. Were Jews now the wealthy patricians whose palaces of consumption at the crossroads of downtown shaped elite tastes? These Jews resided in mansions in suburban residential districts miles from downtown, owned automobiles with chauffeurs, and had large real estate holdings in the central business district. Or were Jews the heavily accented immigrants whose secondhand stores near the waterfront served a politically threatening and ethnically "polluting" working class? To the middle class that now commuted to work on trolley cars, the more numerous immigrant Jews and their families symbolized neighborhoods of racially alien foreigners. This new ethnic clustering suggested that western cities now embodied the cultural alienation and class conflicts of a Milwaukee rather than the deference to mercantile leadership that had characterized a Portland, Los Angeles, or Denver twenty years before. No wonder the elite women of San Francisco's Emanu-El Sisterhood of Personal Service feared that poor immigrants begging on the streets "as if they were in Warsaw" would bring the entire Jewish community into disrepute with wealthy gentiles.[76]

By World War I the pioneer network of Jewish merchants and supply agents still existed in attenuated form. But it had been eclipsed on the one hand by a corporate managerial elite and on the other by a far larger number of aspiring retailers sustaining a new ethnic community. The political culture that had welcomed most merchants—except the Chinese—as comrades in the search for civic stability now recognized class and ethnicity as the urban poles of social conflict. No wonder Harold Hirsch of Meier & Frank faced exclusion from elite gentile men's clubs, which constituted for him and others like him a new and disturbing "anti-Semitism."[77]

NOTES

1. Robert E. Levinson, *The Jews in the California Gold Rush* (New York: KTAV Publishing House, 1978), 20, 29–32.

2. Henry Tobias, *The Jews of New Mexico* (Albuquerque: University of New Mexico Press, 1990), 65–67, 71.

3. Sander L. Gilman and Milton Shain, eds., *Jewries at the Frontier: Accommodation, Identity, Conflict* (Urbana: University of Illinois Press, 1999), includes essays describing the role of Jewish frontier merchants in South Africa, Australia, Brazil, and elsewhere, but nowhere was economic achievement translated into the civic status and political influence that Jews acquired in the American West.

4. Bailey Gatzert interview, 1887, H. H. Bancroft Papers, Bancroft Library, University of California, Berkeley.

5. The advertisement for the Merchants & Farmers Bank in the first Los Angeles city directory in 1872 stated that it issued its own notes. The "accidental" formation of early banks by merchants who issued circulating notes against commodities is discussed in Ron Chernow, *The Death of the Banker* (New York: Vintage Books, 1997), 9–10. Chernow here describes the origins of the Rothschild banks.

6. Harris Newmark, *Sixty Years in Southern California, 1853–1913*, ed. Maurice H. Newmark and Marco Newmark (New York: Knickerbocker Press, 1916), 477; Albert Vorspan and Lloyd P. Gartner, *History of the Jews of Los Angeles* (San Marino, Calif.: Huntington Library, 1970), 39, 41–42.

7. Bailey Gatzert interview.

8. Seattle Public Schools Web site, www.seattleschools.org/. Another school was named in honor of his business partner, Nathan Eckstein.

9. Harriet Lane Levy, *920 O'Farrell Street* (Garden City, New York: Doubleday and Company Inc., 1947), 12, 160.

10. Leslie Page Moch, *Moving Europeans, Migration in Western Europe since 1650* (Bloomington: Indiana University Press, 1992), 16, 32, 103–11, 121.

11. Mark Wyman, *Round-trip to America: The Immigrants Return to Europe, 1880–1930* (Ithaca: Cornell University Press, 1993), 41, 131–37.

12. B. deVries, *From Peddlers to Textile Barons, the Economic Development of a Jewish Minority Group in the Netherlands* (Amsterdam: North Holland, 1989), 92–95, 104, 109, 127–28.

13. Newmark, *Sixty Years in Southern California*, 3–6.

14. Moch, *Moving Europeans*, 148.

15. Newmark, *Sixty Years in Southern California*, 12–26.

16. Ibid., 122.

17. Timothy J. Hatton and Jeffrey G. Williamson, *The Age of Mass Migration: Causes and Economic Impact* (New York: Oxford University Press, 1998), 16, 40. This study examines the complex long-term causes of immigration. The authors emphasize the correlation in locales like the German states between high birthrates and immigration to America twenty years later as well as between the rate of urbanization in Germany and increased rates of immigration to American cities, until the 1890s, when wage rates in the two locales converged.

18. Bernard Goldsmith interview, H. H. Bancroft Papers, Bancroft Library, University of California, Berkeley.

19. Newmark, *Sixty Years in Southern California*, 75-76, 248, 311.

20. Roger Waldinger, *Still the Promised City? African-Americans and New Immigrants in Postindustrial New York* (Cambridge: Harvard University Press, 1996), 255–99.

21. Newmark, *Sixty Years in Southern California*, 140–41; Peter Decker, "Jewish Merchants in San Francisco: Social Mobility on the Urban Frontier," in *The Jews of the West: The Metropolitan Years*, ed. Moses Rischin (Berkeley: Western Jewish History Center of the Judah L. Magnes Memorial Museum, 1979), 14–15.

22. Data gathered from the *Federal Manuscript Census*, Multnomah County, Oregon, 1880.

23. Sylvan Durkheimer interview, 3 March 1975, Oregon Jewish Historical Society, Portland.

24. Newmark, *Sixty Years in Southern California*, 240, 343, 408, 451.

25. An advertisement for S. H. Friendly in the 1892 *Eugene and Lane County Directory* listed him as a hop buyer, but he dealt also in wheat and wool. The list of taxpayers in the directory lists him at $16,150, four times more than any other Jewish taxpayer. Data on Charles Friendly was gathered from the *Federal Manuscript Census*, Multnomah County, Oregon, 1880, and Portland city directories.

26. William Cronon, *Nature's Metropolis: Chicago and the Great West* (New York: W. W. Norton, 1991), 104–5.

27. Newmark, *Sixty Years in Southern California*, 128.

28. Ben Selling to B. Scheeline, 14 April 1883; Selling to Gus Winckler, 31 January and ? March 1883, Ben Selling Papers, Oregon Historical Society, Portland. Wholesalers in San Francisco who supplied general stores in the mining region expected payment in gold dust or nuggets. See Levinson, *The Jews in the California Gold Rush*, 53–55.

29. Ben Selling to "Uncle," 4 July 1886, Selling Papers.

30. Decker, "Jewish Merchants in San Francisco," 19.

31. Ben Selling to "Leo," 25 August 1883; Selling to W. K. Tichnor, 23 February 1883; Selling to "Uncle," 10 September and 12 December 1883; Selling to Gus Winckler, 9 August and 14 November 1883, Selling Papers.

32. Levy, *920 O'Farrell Street*, 163; Ben Selling to J. H. Lunn, 23 December 1883; Selling to father, 24 December 1883, Selling Papers.

33. Harriet Rochlin and Fred Rochlin, *Pioneer Jews: A New Life in the Far West* (Boston: Houghton Mifflin Company, 1984), 130–31.

34. Harold Hirsch interviews, 7 and 26 July, 13 August 1977, Jewish Historical Society of Oregon, Portland.

35. Newmark, *Sixty Years in Southern California*, 248, 287.

36. Data derived from *Federal Manuscript Census*, Linn County, Oregon, 1880.

37. Data on the Gradwohls and Cohns was derived from the *Federal Manuscript Censuses* for Linn County, Oregon; Los Angeles County, California; Storey County, Nevada (all 1880); and Newmark, *Sixty Years in Southern California*, 353, 451.

38. Levy, *920 O'Farrell Street*, 156.

39. Alice Gerstle Levison interview, 1967, H. H. Bancroft Papers, Bancroft Library. University of California, Berkeley.

40. Lena Kleinberg Holzman interview, 23 August 1981, Jewish Community Project, University of Washington Archives, Seattle.

41. The decline of the total fertility rate of white American women in the nineteenth century is summarized in Joseph F. Kett, *Rites of Passage, Adolescence in America, 1790 to the Present* (New York: Basic Books, Inc., 1977), 115. This rate fell from 7.04 births to 3.56 births between 1800 and 1900. The 1880 census does not provide data to compute such a statistic. The 1910 census does allow one to determine the number of children ever born to married women, and by then the daughters of pioneer women were marrying at a higher age and having far fewer children than their mothers. See William Toll, "Jewish Families and the Intergenerational Transition in the American Hinterland," *Journal of American Ethnic History* 12, no. 2 (winter 1993), 27 (table 12).

42. William Toll, *The Making of an Ethnic Middle Class: Portland Jewry over Four Generations* (Albany: State University of New York Press, 1982), 49.

43. Newmark, *Sixty Years in Southern California*, 334–35, 470, 515.

44. Data derived from federal manuscript censuses.

45. Levy, *920 O'Farrell Street*.

46. Jewish families of Albany and Eugene organized a joint religious congregation in 1878. Among the first officers and trustees were merchants from Albany, Eugene, Corvallis, and Harrisburg. See Minutes and Miscellaneous Correspondence of the First Hebrew Congregation of Albany, Oregon, 1878–1924, American Jewish Archives, Cincinnati.

47. Street maps of Eugene, Albany, Portland, Tacoma, Seattle, and Virginia City for various years in the late nineteenth century are available at the Map Library of the University of Oregon and the Map Library of the University of Washington. The addresses of businesses are given in the city directories of the respective cities, and home addresses are usually provided in the federal manuscript censuses. The location of stores and houses can usually be traced to specific blocks, if not to specific buildings on the block.

48. Newmark, *Sixty Years in Southern California*, 121.

49. Data on the stores was derived from *The First Los Angeles City and County Directory, 1872* (Los Angeles: Ward Ritchie Press, 1963), and the elevated map of Los Angeles available at the Map Library, University of Oregon.

50. Jonathan Sarna, "The Mythical Jew and the Jew Next Door in Nineteenth-Century America," in *Anti-Semitism in American History*, ed. David A. Gerber (Urbana: University of Illinois Press, 1986), 57–78.

51. Levy, *920 O'Farrell Street*, 230. Data on the shops of Meyer and his brother were derived from *Federal Manuscript Census*, Virginia City, 1880.

52. Decker, "Jewish Merchants in San Francisco," 13.

53. I. J. Benjamin, *Three Years in America*, vol. 2 (Philadelphia: Jewish Publication Society, 1956), 9, 25, 28, 36, 42, 49, 64.

54. Fred Rosenbaum, *Architects of Reform: Congregational and Community Leadership, Emanu-El of San Francisco, 1849–1980* (Berkeley: Judah L. Magnes Memorial Museum, 1980), 30–32.

55. Toll, *Making of an Ethnic Middle Class*, 23, 32 (map).

56. *Trinidad Directory for the Year 1892* (Trinidad, Colorado: Bensel Directory Company, 1892), 16–17.

57. Hasia R. Diner, *A Time for Gathering: The Second Migration, 1820–1880*, vol. 2 of *The Jewish People in America* (Baltimore: Johns Hopkins University Press, 1992), 109.

58. Michael Zarchin, *Glimpses of Jewish Life in San Francisco*, rev. ed. (Berkeley: Judah L. Magnes Memorial Museum, 1964), 168–70.

59. Data collected from *Seattle City Directory for 1897* (Seattle: Polk's Seattle Directory Co., 1897).

60. Toll, *Making of an Ethnic Middle Class*, 31–36.

61. Tony Fels, "'The Non-Evangelical Alliance': Freemasonry in Gilded-Age San Francisco," in *Religion and Society in the American West: Historical Essays*, ed. Carl Guarneri and David Alvarez (Lanham, Md.: University Press of America, 1987), 240–41. Fels concludes that the proportion of Jews in the Masonic lodges equaled their percentage in the city's non-Catholic male population.

62. Newmark, *Sixty Years in Southern California*, 26, 75, 203; Toll, *Making of an Ethnic Middle Class*, 91.

63. David C. Hammack, "Small Business and Urban Power: Some Notes on the History of Economic Policy in Nineteenth-Century American Cities," in *Small Business in American Life*, ed. Stuart Bruchey (New York: Columbia University Press, 1980), 320–21.

64. Edwin McDowell, *Barry Goldwater, Portrait of an Arizonan* (Chicago: Henry Regnery Company, 1964), 40–42.

65. Toll, *Making of an Ethnic Middle Class*, 85–86.

66. Rochlin and Rochlin, *Pioneer Jews*, 84–86; William Toll, "Pioneering: Jewish Men and Women of the American West," in *Creating American Jews, Historical Conversations about Identity* (Hanover, N.H.: University Press of New England, 1998), 27.

67. On the extraordinary change in consumption in urban America in the early twentieth century and the special role of huge stores like Marshall Field's, Carson Pirie Scott, and especially Wanamaker's, see William Leach, *Land of Desire, Merchants, Power, and the Rise of a New American Culture* (New York: Pantheon Books, 1993), 20–35.

68. Tobias, *The Jews of New Mexico*, 113.

69. Ezra and Joy Hana Menashe interview, Jewish Historical Society of Oregon, Portland.

70. Seattle had a forty-two-story skyscraper, the L. C. Smith Tower, at Second and Yesler Way—a Jewish, Italian, and Japanese area—as early as 1914. See Sydney LeBlanc, *Twentieth-Century American Architecture: A Traveler's Guide to 220 Key Buildings* (New York: Whitney Library of Design, 1996), 25.

71. In all fairness, a letterhead of the Golden Eagle Dry Goods Company in 1936 shows a large, five-story masonry building at Fifth and Lawrence, although it still specialized in wholesale and retail dry goods, not a full line of merchandise like the largest department stores.

72. For the changes in the legal classification of urban property that department stores brought about, see Max Gage, *The Creative Destruction of Manhattan, 1900–1940* (Chicago: University of Chicago Press, 1999), 23–31.

73. Harold Hirsch interview.

74. Information about the location of department stores for the various cities is located in city directories.

75. For the changeover nationally from partnership to incorporation, see Leach, *Land of Desire*, 17–19.

76. "Employment Department," *Third Annual Report of the Emanu-El Sisterhood for Fiscal Year 1896–97* (San Francisco, 1897), 11, 17.

77. Harold Hirsch interview.

Mandelkern & Dombrow   183 ESSEX ST.
                               COR. HOUSTON ST.
                                        N.Y.

From Cooperative Farming to Urban Leadership

Ellen Eisenberg

I N 1882 A GROUP OF approximately forty Jews, recently arrived from Russia, traveled from New York to Portland, Oregon, via Panama. From there they journeyed 250 miles overland through the Willamette Valley to Roseburg, where they purchased more than 760 acres of land and incorporated as the New Odessa Community. Renouncing any claim to private property, the cooperative dedicated itself to communal living, agricultural pursuits, and "mutual assistance in perfecting and development of physical, mental, and moral capacities of its members."[1]

About a decade later, Rachel Kahn journeyed from Russia to New York as a picture bride. She married Abraham Calof in New York, and the young couple traveled by train to North Dakota, where they joined a decade-old Jewish farming settlement at Devils Lake. Braving subzero temperatures, blizzards, and a fearsome mother-in–law, and living in a twelve-by-fourteen-foot shack that housed six people, a flock of chickens, and a cow, Rachel and her new husband set themselves to their new work as Jewish farmers in America.

Any student of American Jewish history would expect to find small communities of German Jewish merchants in places like Roseburg, Oregon, and Devils Lake, North Dakota. Such merchants first appeared in the American West in the mid-nineteenth century, many of them settling down after careers as itinerant peddlers. Yet, as the stories of the New Odessa Community and Rachel Calof suggest, these rural, western settings were also home to something unexpected: agrarian colonies of Russian Jews.

William Frey, leader of the New Odessa Community, and his wife. Courtesy of the Jacob Rader Marcus Center of the American Jewish Archives, Cincinnati.

In the early 1880s a flood of eastern European Jewish immigrants began pouring into American ports. Crowding in the immigrant districts of eastern cities and the specter of anti-Semitism led several American Jewish leaders, like the New York banker Jacob Schiff, to tout the prospect of Jewish settlement in the West. Relatively few of the "new" Jewish immigrants looked for opportunities there, though. Even San Francisco, where German Jewish settlement in the mid-nineteenth century created the second-largest Jewish community in America, did not attract large numbers of eastern Europeans.

A small but determined contingent of aspiring farmers, however, did sojourn or settle in western colonies, many of them inspired by agrarian, socialist, and enlightenment ideologies and dedicated to proving the viability of collective settlement and the productivity of the Jewish laborer. Jewish farm settlements like New Odessa were established in western states, including California, Oregon, the Dakotas, Kansas, Minnesota, Colorado, and Utah. While these colonies often folded within a few years, their settlers helped to create nuclei for Jewish communities in remote areas of the West and to shape the identity of several important western Jewish communities. As the story of Joseph Nudelman, one of the most determined Jewish colonists, demonstrates, even failed cooperative experiments could create migration streams that affected Jewish settlement patterns and provided the participants with valuable experiences and tools for urban leadership.

Early in 1882, Nudelman arrived in the United States from Russia and began an odyssey that would lead him through Colorado, North Dakota, California, Nevada, and Oregon. Unlike the German Jewish merchants who had preceded him, he was not driven by commercial aspirations, nor did he share the independent dream of the American homesteader. Rather, his wanderings in the West were part of his repeated attempts to fulfill his dream of establishing a Jewish agricultural colony.

Born in Odessa in 1844, Nudelman, the oldest of nine children, spent his early adulthood working as a merchant in southern Russia and Rumania. By 1881 he had determined that his future lay neither in Russia nor in trade, and he began to seek opportunities for agricultural colonization. In 1881 he organized two groups of colonists. The first left for Canada that year; the second, which included Nudelman, his wife and four children, two of his siblings and their families, and at least five other families, sailed a year later.[2]

Nudelman's odyssey took him first to Canada, where he met with members of the earlier group. After returning to New York and meeting

114

with potential financial sponsors, including Jacob Schiff, Nudelman led the group to Colorado, where they worked on the railroads and in the silver mines, saving money to buy farmland. In 1883 they filed claims on land in McClean County, North Dakota. Nudelman's group was not alone in seeing potential in the Dakotas; his colony, Painted Woods, joined the Devils Lake community in North Dakota and two others that had been established in South Dakota the previous year.

All these settlements were products of a growing "back to the soil" movement centered in the Southern Pale of Russia. Frustrated by continued repression by Russian authorities, many Jews became enamored of revolutionary ideologies. In south Russia, where there was a relatively large concentration of secularly educated Jewish university students, many were attracted to Russian agrarian and socialist ideologies. The eruption of anti-Jewish pogroms centered there in 1881–82 led many of these intellectuals and revolutionaries to reassess their commitment to fighting for their rights in Russia. Many decided to apply their socialist and agrarian ideals on more fertile soil, in Palestine or the American West.

Those idealists who set their sights on America formed the Am Olam in Odessa in 1881. This group combined elements of many of the movements competing for members during this period of crisis for Russian Jews. Like advocates of the Jewish enlightenment movement known as the *Haskalah*, Am Olam participants believed that secularism and alteration of the "abnormal" Jewish occupational structure was the key to emancipation and acceptance. Like many in the emergent Zionist movement, Am Olam advocates had concluded that there was no future for Jews in Russia. Many in the movement also embraced revolutionary ideologies, dedicating themselves to communal settlements that would serve as a precursor to a larger socialist revolution.[3]

Beginning in 1881, between six and twelve Am Olam groups departed for the United States to establish a network of agricultural colonies. Ultimately, approximately seventy communities, ranging in size from a few dozen to 2,500 people, were formed, many in the West. While most of these colonies cannot be directly linked to the Am Olam, threads of the group's ideology were apparent in virtually every one.

At Bethlehem Judea, a settlement founded in South Dakota by an Am Olam group organized in the southern Russian city of Kremenchug, members lived together as one household, and all property was held communally. The settlers made their lofty aims clear in their constitution: "The colony Bethlehem Judea is founded . . . to help the Jewish people in its emancipation from slavery and in its rehabilitation to a new truth, free-

Samuel Sack, in Russian worker's cap, riding a disk harrow at Clarion Colony, Utah, c. 1913. From the Archives of *Western States Jewish History.*

dom, and peace. The colony shall demonstrate to the enemies of our people the world over that Jews are capable of farming."[4] This belief that normalization and productiveness through agricultural labor would solve the "Jewish problem" was shared in many colonies. As Herman Rosenthal, leader of colonization attempts at Sicily Island, Louisiana, and Cremieux, South Dakota, explained: "Long ago I had come to the conclusion that so long as we have no toiling class that produces its own bread there will be no end to our tribulations. A people that lives at the expense of the labor of others cannot continue to exist indefinitely. Similarly the Jewish problem will not be solved by the non-Jewish world. . . . In my opinion, one of the best means of averting this danger would be to establish a class of half a million farmers and workers living by the sweat of their brows."[5]

A number of the colonies founded in the early 1880s, including Bethlehem Judea and New Odessa, were settled on communally owned land. In these colonies, this cooperative arrangement was intended to be lasting and thorough and included shared housing and dining. In other cases, particularly in later settlements like Utah's Clarion Colony , members intended to farm together initially and to later separate the land into individual holdings. In a number of colonies, including Cremieux, South Dakota, several Kansas colonies, and Cotopaxi, Colorado, where land was obtained under the Homestead Act, individuals held land, but social and cultural activities, and even many economic functions, were cooperative.

In addition to stressing agricultural labor and communalism, many colonies emphasized democratic values and a commitment to self-improvement. The New Odessa Community's Articles of Incorporation, for example, declared that the colony's object was "mutual assistance in perfecting and development of physical, mental, and moral capacities of its members."[6] Likewise, Bethlehem Judea's constitution declared that the colony was dedicated "to the improvement of the moral and intellectual condition of its members and their families, to promote their welfare by united and harmonious action on their part and to afford mutual assistance to themselves."[7] The emphasis on morality was severed from religion in many of these colonies. Visiting rabbis bemoaned the lack of religious observance in several places, and colonists not only ignored but flouted Jewish law by raising pigs.

The emphasis on moral improvement was very strongly embraced in the New Odessa Community, where a non-Jewish leader, William Frey, was recruited to provide moral and intellectual leadership. One colonist explained the schedule:

> We work from 6:00 in the morning till half-past 8 in the morning. . . . Then we have breakfast. Work is resumed at 10:00 and continued to 4:00 in the afternoon. [Next] is dinner, followed by a rest period and intellectual activity. Monday, Tuesday, Thursday, and Friday are devoted to the study of mathematics, English and to Frey's lecture on the philosophy of positivism. On Wednesday, current matters are discussed and on Saturday the problems of the commune. On Sunday we rise . . . and immediately a lively discussion begins on the subject of equal rights for women. . . . After breakfast, one member goes to survey the farm, another reads a newspaper or a book, the rest sing, shout and dance. [Later] dinner is served. Two men wash the dishes, the choir sings, the organ plays. . . . [Then] begins a session of mutual criticism; then the work for the week is assigned.[8]

While surviving constitutions provide a fairly clear sense of Am Olam colonies like Bethlehem Judea and New Odessa, relatively little is known about daily life at many others, such as Nudelman's Painted Woods. Still, the timing of the settlement, the origins of the settlers, and the emphasis on the collective make it clear that it was part of the same general movement. Like the socialist agrarians who settled in 1882 in Bethlehem Judea and New Odessa, Nudelman and his comrades were of South Pale origin and left Russia in the same period. Their determination to establish an agrarian settlement was noted by the St. Paul sponsors, who found that "nothing but land could satisfy them."[9] This was a collective rather than an individual endeavor; the core group was organized in Russia prior to departure and remained intact through the sojourn in Colorado and for approximately three to six years in North Dakota. Indeed, the collective emphasis of the group brought them into conflict with their American neighbors. As a McClean County Historical Society publication explains, "The Russian Jews at the Painted Woods colony continued to remain huddled together on the school section in the village of New Jerusalem and would not go separately and establish homes on the claims they had filed on, until a petition signed by 25 American neighbors all within a distance of five miles, requested their removal from this school section to their own land holdings, was officially executed August, 1882." The neighbors' complaint, which was laced with a variety of anti-Semitic stereotypes and

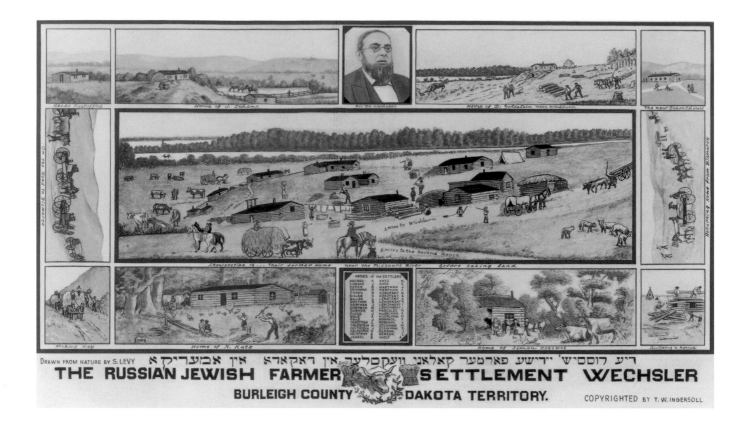

DRAWN FROM NATURE BY S. LEVY

א דאקארא אין וועקסלער קאלאני פארמער ידישע רוסיש׳ ריע

THE RUSSIAN JEWISH FARMER SETTLEMENT WECHSLER

BURLEIGH COUNTY DAKOTA TERRITORY.

COPYRIGHTED BY T. W. INGERSOLL

The Painted Woods settlement, also known as the Wechsler Colony (after Rabbi Wechsler), c. 1880s. Courtesy of the Jacob Rader Marcus Center of the American Jewish Archives, Cincinnati.

accusations, led to a visit by Rabbi Judah Wechsler of Minnesota, who gave the colonists "a very emphatic notice that they must go on their own lands and behave themselves, or leave the country."[10]

A set of drawings of Painted Woods (also known as the Wechsler Colony, after Rabbi Wechsler) shows a tight settlement of houses along the Missouri River. While the creation of this village aroused suspicion among neighboring farmers, this pattern of settlement is an indication of the collective mission of the immigrants. Several pictures show the settlers traveling together by wagon back and forth from Bismarck and working together to build houses and bale hay. A centerpiece, listing the names of all the settlers, reinforces the clear message that this was a colony—a group endeavor—not simply a collection of individuals.

Nudelman's central role in the colony is acknowledged in several sources. The Nudelman family history depicts him as the organizer and leader of the group as the members sojourned in Colorado prior to settlement in North

The Nudelman family outside their house in Wellington, Nevada, 1895. Courtesy of the Oregon Jewish Museum, Portland.

Dakota. His leadership is confirmed in local land records, which indicate that the Painted Woods colonists planned a second village, to be called Nudelman. The McClean County deed was filed in May of 1888, and the town's site platted, although these plans never became a reality. Nudelman's leadership was also recognized when he was elected treasurer of the newly created Montefiore school district.[11]

While documentation about the structure of the Painted Woods colony is lacking, tales of the hardships faced by settlers there are not. As a Nudelman family history recalls: "Many stories have been told of the hardships of survival in the colony. In nine years there was only one really good crop. Joseph told many times of the severe winters in North Dakota. During most of the winters it snowed so hard that snow was banked up to the roof when the blizzard winds blew. The cattle barns were also covered and it was necessary to tunnel from the house to the barn in order to reach the cattle and feed them."[12] Despite these hardships, by 1889 at least thirteen colony families had completed the five years necessary to gain full title to their homesteads.[13]

While the difficulties faced by the Nudelman family and their comrades in North Dakota soured many on the prospect of agricultural settlement, Nudelman remained undaunted. After leaving the colony and spending a year in Portland, he "still had a yearning to be a farmer and colonize in another area."[14] Journeying to San Francisco, he was reunited with a Mr. Katz, one of the members of the North Dakota community who had journeyed from Russia with him. Nudelman and Katz, along with Nudelman's brothers Phillip and Israel, became the core of a second colony, near Porterville in Tulare County, California. Soon, fifteen to twenty families resided there. In contrast to their North Dakota experience, where cold was the most bitter enemy, the families struggled in Porterville with heat and a lack of fresh water.

Joseph Nudelman and wife Fanny, c. 1915. Courtesy of the Oregon Jewish Museum, Portland.

The Porterville colony, which lasted less than two years, was only the first of three attempts by Nudelman to farm in California. After two years in Porterville, most of the families left, and Nudelman moved on to Orangevale, where he worked in an orchard until he was badly injured in a fall. Following a brief sojourn in San Francisco, where several members of the Nudelman family now lived, Nudelman attempted a short-lived partnership on a farm near Heywood. Despite these three unsuccessful California ventures, an undaunted Nudelman, along with brothers Israel, Samuel, and Phillip, brother-in-law Moishe, and sons Sam and Maurice, tried again in 1897, purchasing a ranch of more than five thousand acres in Nevada. Like his earlier ventures, this proved unsuccessful. Finally, in late 1902, Nudelman and his family moved to San Francisco and then on to Portland.

Although he had been so determined to farm, Nudelman found more success in the city. When the Painted Woods colony had dissolved due to crop failures and increasing debt in the mid-1880s, many of its member families—now intertwined by marriages—had journeyed together to Portland. Nudelman joined this network of siblings and in-laws in small business ventures. His meat market stood next door to his brother Sam's grocery store. Other family members opened scrap metal, picture framing, dry goods, feed, and cartage businesses. Nudelman quickly became a community leader in Portland, serving as the founding president of its first Orthodox synagogue, Shaarie Torah, and as a founder of the Jewish Old People's Home.

Although Nudelman's efforts to establish Jewish agricultural colonies continued into the 1890s, most Jews who settled on western farms after the 1880s acted as individuals rather than as members of colonies. Nevertheless, several scattered collective ventures were founded in later years. For example, the Russian immigrant Benjamin Brown founded Clarion Colony in Utah in 1911. Convinced that his cooperative would serve as a model for the establishment of a network of settlements, he hoped to recruit more than a hundred families to invest in land that they were to work communally first before dividing it among themselves. Ultimately, Brown intended that the community would combine private land holdings with cooperative buying and selling. While he succeeded in settling 156 people on thirty-six farms, floods devastated the experiment, and the land was sold to creditors within a few years.[15]

While Clarion was founded several decades after the primary period of Jewish agricultural colonization in the American West, that community's natural disaster was a telling emblem for this movement. Unlike their eastern counterparts in New Jersey, which persisted into the 1920s, the western colonies were all short-lived. Settlements in the Dakotas suffered through droughts, blizzards, thunderstorms, hail, and prairie fires. A number of colonies, including those in Kansas and Utah, lacked adequate water for crops. In the most ideological of the colonies, Bethlehem Judea and New Odessa, communal living arrangements led to tensions and disagreements. At Bethlehem Judea, disputes over work assignments led settlers to divide the colony into private holdings after eighteen months. At New Odessa, tensions between followers and detractors of William Frey, combined with a fire that destroyed the community building and library, led to the demise of the colony.

Land policies in America also worked against communal settlements. The colonists at Nudelman's Painted Woods were not the only ones whose attempts to create a cooperative ran afoul of local norms and practices. For example, when veterans of the community venture at Sicily Island, Louisiana, seeking a cooler climate, decided to establish a colony in South Dakota, they were compelled to stake out individual claims under the Homestead Act, which did not make allowances for group ownership.

Besides ideological disputes and natural disasters, problems relating to financing and sponsorship unraveled many colonies. As Nudelman's repeated efforts to obtain support from sponsors illustrate, aspiring colonists were often long on idealism but short on funds. To secure land and supplies, groups turned to Jewish philanthropists, many of whom saw colonies as a way of "removing" newcomers from crowded urban districts. Sponsors also hoped that agricultural colonies would help to "normalize" the immigrants by making them productive farmers. Both "removal" and "normalization" were seen as effective strategies for countering the anti-Semitism that had increased as the number of Jewish immigrants rose. Thus, philanthropists sponsored colonies for reasons of their own and often came into conflict with the settlers they were helping.[16]

An excellent example can be seen in the Kansas colony of Beersheba, sponsored by a group led by Rabbi Isaac Mayer Wise of Cincinnati. Convinced that the colonists needed supervision, the Cincinnati sponsors hired agents to travel with and supervise the colony. Tensions between the colonists and the agents soon led to resentment and, ultimately, open hostility. Colonists claimed that the sponsor-appointed supervisor ruled "with terror" and expelled colonists from the settlement at will. When colonists began to act independently by leasing part of their land to a cattle syndicate, the sponsors punished them by taking away all their possessions. Ultimately, the Beersheba colonists became convinced that there was more opportunity for them in business than farming, and many left the settlement to become merchants in various Kansas cities.[17]

Even where relations with sponsors were more congenial, as at Painted Woods, the colony's failure to thrive economically led to sponsor disillusionment and frustration. Rabbi Wechsler rallied St. Paul Jews to support the colonists and even wrote a letter, published in the *Washburn Times* on 11 October 1883, defending the settlers against accusations. Yet even his defense illustrated the gap between the American sponsors and the immigrant colonists: "The Russian Jew is far inferior to the Jews of other countries so far as culture and refinement are concerned, owing largely to the fact that they have not enjoyed the benefits of a good education. Here these poor, ill-treated Jews should receive all encouragement possible. With all their faults and shortcomings they are lawabiding [*sic*], industrious, and frugal, and will become good and useful citizens of this blessed land of freedom."

The paternalistic attitude of sponsors like Wechsler reinforced their tendency to blame the colonists when settlements failed. While colonies were plagued by the same natural disasters, low crop prices, and mechanization and debt issues that triggered a rural to urban migration in late-nineteenth-century America, sponsors tended to blame colony failures on the settlers' shortcomings. When members left debt-ridden cooperatives to seek better opportunities in nearby cities, sponsors regarded them as failures.

Within a decade of the initial settlements, financial sponsors, many of whom had regarded their aid as an investment from which they hoped to earn a return, had concluded that such collective ventures were doomed, and they decided to aid only individual farmers. In contrast to the sponsors' assessments, examination of the legacy of the settlements demonstrates that the colonists' toil in rural, western America was not for naught. First, for Nudelman and many other colony veterans, their experiences provided skills that proved useful in urban settings. In addition, in areas where colonization had been fairly extensive, such as North Dakota, the colonies opened the area to continued Jewish settlement on farms and in small towns in the area. Focusing on settler accounts like Nudelman's, and on regional, rather than colony, histories, illuminates the ways in which the colonization program left a lasting impression on both the settlers and on several western Jewish communities.

Published accounts of Painted Woods, for example, tend to focus on the sponsors' role in the colony and to treat the settlers in a cursory or negative manner. In contrast to Nudelman's account, in which the colonists themselves organize the migration, scout for land, and administer the settlement, published histories give almost sole credit for the community to Rabbi Wechsler. Accounts in *North Dakota History* state clearly that the rabbi was "largely responsible for the agricultural colony's becoming a reality."[18] Such histories trace Wechsler's continued aid over several years and his growing disillusionment, ending with the demise of the colony in 1886 and Wechsler's decision to resign his St. Paul pulpit. The fates of the colonists—none of whom are discussed as individuals—are not explored. Similarly, published accounts of the California and Nevada settlements depict the sponsors as the primary actors.

The Nudelman family history, by contrast, states that by 1893, "after spending about a year in Portland, Joseph still had a yearning to be a farmer and colonize in another area." According to this account, Nudelman traveled to San Francisco, where he had connections with family members and former colonists, including Mr. Katz. Once in San Francisco, Nudelman and Katz went to see "Mr. Linentaul," obtained his financial backing, and selected the land for the colony themselves. Published, historical accounts, however, credit the philanthropist Philip Lilienthal and San Francisco's Rabbi Voorsanger with the settlement of Porterville.[19] Indeed, press accounts asserted that Lilienthal brought fifteen families from the Dakotas to Porterville, a claim that tends to exaggerate the role of the sponsors and make the colonists sound more dependent and less capable.[20]

Nudelman's account shows that after a brief period in Orangevale, a settlement established a few years earlier by others, Nudelman was joined by Phillip, Israel, Samuel, Moishe, Sam, and Maurice Nudelman, a collection of brothers and sons, at Wymore Ranch in Nevada. While the family history documents the decision of these relatives to purchase this ranch together, an account of the colony published in 1891 depicts this effort as having been led entirely by local philanthropists who went to San Francisco to recruit the seventeen families involved. In this case, however, published accounts do make clear that the so-called philanthropists were motivated by self-interest and that ultimately the settlers, led by Nudelman, succeeded in purchasing the land at a fraction of the price suggested by the sponsor.[21]

The Nudelman family history—a rare account from the point of view of the settlers—serves as a useful corrective to histories based on the assertions of sponsors who were disappointed that their investment in agricultural colonies had not paid off. The family history gets beyond the issue of colony success or failure to present quite a different picture of the settlers and their experience. First, since the account begins in Russia, with the listing of the families involved, and follows the various intertwined family groups through to their final destination in Portland, it illuminates the group experience. The interconnections among the families are elucidated, as are the ways in which these connections persisted over generations after the demise of the colony. Clearly, while the agricultural venture may have failed, the group solidarity persisted.

The settlers' accounts also show their initiative and suggest the sort of skills and abilities necessary for colony leadership. The Nudelman history documents him traveling independently, securing financial backing, and making land deals. Primary sources such as articles of incorporation filed by colonists, purchase agreements, and other legal documents confirm the impression of competence that the family history suggests.

In addition, the focus on the family's ventures after leaving the community demonstrates the way in which the colony experience fostered the adjustment of the settlers and helped provide them with skills that could be applied later. Spending several years in rural America afforded the colonists an opportunity to learn English, which enabled them to enter established, urban American Jewish communities more quickly upon their arrival in cities. They also gained experience negotiating land deals, dealing with bankers, serving as elected public officials, and organizing several large groups, skills that contributed to Nudelman's ability to spearhead the organization of a religious congregation and construction of a synagogue within a few years of his arrival in Portland.

In moving from colony to urban leadership, Nudelman was fairly typical of a large cohort of commune veterans who arrived in Portland. At least eighteen families spent time in the Dakotas prior to their arrival in Portland, and at least fourteen of them were members of the Painted Woods colony.[22] These families were instrumental in the establishment of the key institutions serving the new eastern European Jewish community in south Portland. For example, a group of Painted Woods colonists who arrived in Portland in the late 1880s were the principal founders of Congregation Neveh Zedek. One of these leaders was Marcus Gale, a Painted Woods veteran who farmed in Oregon City for several years before settling in Portland. Gale not only served as Neveh Zedek's president for a total of eighteen years, he also played an active role in the Republican Party in Portland.

Nor was the North Dakota colony the only one to provide leaders to Portland. Zachary Swett journeyed with his family to Oregon as part of the group that established the strictly communal, agrarian settlement of New Odessa. His son Isaac became one of the most prominent Jewish leaders in

Portland. Joining Ahavai Shalom, Swett became a congregational leader as well as a prominent B'nai B'rith activist. Max Levin, who spent several years in rural Kansas, was one of the principal organizers of Congregation Talmud Torah.

Painted Woods veterans also became leaders of other key Jewish institutions in Portland. Hirsch Lauterstein was one of several former North Dakotans to provide leadership roles at Congregation Ahavai Shalom. Likewise, Israel Bromberg, brother-in-law of both Nudelman and Lauterstein, was instrumental in establishing the Portland Hebrew School, which served the entire immigrant population of Portland.

The leadership of former colonists fostered the development of a Hebrew School that transmitted to the Jewish children of south Portland the settlers' values. The school emphasized modern instruction and "Hebrew as a language for cultural revitalization."[23] The clear Zionist orientation of the school was intertwined with the founders' devotion to Jewish agrarian pursuits.[24] Historian William Toll notes, "The leading promoters of the Hebrew school were also the leading local sponsors of the United Palestine Appeal with its message of 'Back to the Soil of the Homeland.'"[25] Likewise, Deborah Goldberg notes in her thesis on Zionism in Portland "the correlation of Zionism and frontierism apparent among families who came to Portland from farming colonies in North Dakota. One of the most active and ardent Zionist families, the Bromberg-Lauterstein clan, came to Portland from a Jewish farm in North Dakota. [Israel] Bromberg, for example, served as principal of the Hebrew School and was an important Zionist ideologue whose Zionist editorials frequently appeared in *The Scribe*. Perhaps it is this phenomenon that explains the consistent Zionist activity at Congregation Neveh Tzedek, the synagogue formed by ex-North Dakotan farmers."[26] The influence of these former colonists contributed heavily to the strength of Zionism in Portland, in contrast to the movement's weakness in many other western cities.

Colony veterans also brought to Portland their strong sense of group identity. As Toll notes, "Jews with agrarian ideals . . . reflected a collective rather than a familial sense of social cohesiveness and portended a much stronger ethnic consciousness than had existed among the German Jews of the nineteenth century. . . . A sense of communalism grew with the increased social status of the newcomers who had had some farming experience."[27]

Finally, and not surprisingly, given the relative acculturation of immigrants who had pioneered in rural America, colony veterans helped to promote the rapid Americanization of later immigrants through the institutions they established. The two Russian congregations founded in Portland

Abraham and Rachel Bella Calof with three daughters at Devils Lake, North Dakota, about 1910. Courtesy of the Jewish Historical Society of the Upper Midwest, St. Paul.

in the 1890s promoted themselves as modern, American institutions, reaching out to the larger Jewish community in advertisements that emphasized English-language sermons, organ music, and orderly services. Likewise, the Portland Hebrew School strongly supported the Americanization of its pupils and rejected traditional teaching methods. The creation of a unified school serving the several Conservative and Orthodox congregations of south Portland may also reflect the collectivist tendencies so dear to the colony veterans.

The pattern of movement from colony to urban leadership among these Portland families was replicated in several other western cities. For example, in North Dakota colony veterans contributed significantly to the development of Jewish communities in towns and cities. While German Jewish merchants were the first Jews to settle in many North Dakota towns, eastern Europeans soon outnumbered the earlier arrivals and played critical roles in these communities.[28] Of the four hundred families who filed homestead claims in one of North Dakota's Jewish colonies, some remained in North Dakota as peddlers or urban merchants after abandoning their claims, contributing to the development of Jewish communities. For example, a number of Devils Lake colonists, including their leader Ben Zion Greenberg (after whom the Ben Zion, North Dakota, post office was named), had settled in Grand Forks by 1900. These families were key in the establishment of Grand Forks as the state's first "flourishing and self-conscious Jewish urban community."[29] By the 1880s, the town boasted the state's first rabbi and permanent synagogue, a Hebrew school, Ladies' Aid Society, and *Chevra Kadisha* (Jewish burial society).

Several oral histories taken during the Depression document the movement from western colony to western city. Isak Edelman stated that his father, a native of Kiev, took up a claim in Devils Lake in 1884, along with fifty other settlers. After working on his father's farm throughout his childhood, Edelman entered the hotel business, first in Hansboro, North Dakota, and later in the town of Devils Lake. By the 1930s, Edelman had run an auto business and finally a grocery establishment there. Similarly, Hartz Naftel Katz told of his father's journey to the Dakotas to settle a homestead in 1882, where he farmed for several years. Katz subsequently ran several businesses in Minnesota, finally settling into a drugstore career in Fargo, North Dakota.[30] In Kansas, farmers abandoning the Beersheba colony set up businesses first in nearby Ravanna and later in Dodge City and Kansas City.[31]

The trajectory of settlers from agrarian ventures to urban communities was not the only legacy of the colonies. While the colonies failed to sustain themselves for any length of time, they helped to open remote and unlikely areas of settlement to later arriving Jewish immigrants, including aspiring farmers.

Such continued rural settlement is portrayed vividly in the memoir of Rachel Calof. While several years passed between the demise of the North Dakota colonies and her arrival as a young bride, conditions remained harsh. She tells of blizzards, ruined crops, and indescribable cold. Most vivid is her description of the living conditions she found when she arrived at her in-laws' one-room cabin in 1894:

> We five people . . .were not to have such spacious quarters all to ourselves. At this time the in-laws had a flock of twelve chickens and Abe and I also had twelve. There was no outside coop for the poultry, but if there had been we would have lost the flock in short order because the temperature would soon be going to forty or more degrees below zero and the chickens would have frozen to death. We needed to keep them alive in hopes of having their eggs as

well as their meat later on. Each family was to keep its chickens under its bed and the ends and sides were closed off to form a cage. Also there was a calf which had to be accommodated inside.

    This is how five human beings and twenty-five animals faced the beginning of the savage winter of the plains in a twelve-by-fourteen-foot shack. The chickens were generous with their perfumes and we withstood this, but the stench of the calf tethered in the corner was well-nigh intolerable.[32]

Calof's memoir gives no indication that she was even aware that a colony had existed where she came to settle; indeed, her memoir emphasizes the isolation she felt. However, her family was one of several clustered together near Devils Lake and was served by the circuit-riding Rabbi Benjamin Papermaster.[33]

Common locations and hardships were not the only threads that tied together colonists and the later-arriving individual settlers. While Rachel Calof arrived at the site of the former Devils Lake Colony after it had dissolved, the first member of the extended Calof family to come to North Dakota was Mordechai, a member of the Painted Woods colony.[34] His family, including Rachel's husband, followed later. After giving up farming, some members of the Calof family followed the Nudelman group to Portland.

The North Dakota case demonstrates clearly the way in which these colonies, despite their failure to sustain themselves, opened the door to further Jewish agrarian settlement. The areas that Painted Woods and the other Dakota colonies had pioneered were populated by subsequent waves of Jewish settlers. Veterans of the failing Painted Woods and Devils Lake communities established Iola, twenty miles from Devils Lake, in 1886. After experiencing extreme deprivation, the farmers of this settlement were saved by a national appeal for aid.[35] As some Jewish settlers abandoned the colonies, newcomers replaced them. These new settlers, arriving in North Dakota after the 1880s, came not as colonists but as independent farmers. The failure of colonies like Cremieux, Painted Woods, and Bethlehem Judea led funding agencies to move away from supporting colonies in favor of assisting individual farmers who established clustered settlements, building on what had been left by their predecessors.[36] Thus, the 3 remaining families in Painted Woods at the turn of the century were joined by 40 more by 1906, and the total reached 250 by 1912.[37] By 1919 the North Dakota Development League reported that the state was fourth in the nation (and first in the West) in numbers of Jewish farmers, with many concentrated in the area of the former colonies in the western part of the state.[38] According to a 1986 publication by the North Dakota Institute for Regional Studies, approximately four hundred Jewish settlers filed claims in one of the seven different colonies, while an additional four

Stock certificate for part of a sow, Orangevale Stock Farm Association, 1917. Autry Museum of Western Heritage, Los Angeles.

hundred established "small but distinct clusters of settlement." The early colony activity, according to the same publication, "popularized the idea of coming to the midwestern free-land areas. The publication by the Jewish press of reports of the first settlers brought hundreds of other men and women to the prairies."[39]

This influx of Jewish immigrants had a profound impact on the emerging Jewish communities of the region. In contrast to the conventional wisdom that German Jews dominated communities in the American West well into the twentieth century, the widespread settlement in North Dakota by Jews from the South Pale territories where Am Olam ideologies were strongest gave that state's emerging Jewish community a distinctly south Russian flavor. The scattered German Jewish merchants in North Dakota towns "were joined by homestead men who rather quickly moved to the towns and engaged in business ventures" by the 1890s.[40] When Rabbi Benjamin Papermaster arrived in Grand Forks in 1891, "he found that most of the families were from the Ukraine section of Russia."[41] These south Russians filled a special niche in a state with a very large population of Volga Germans. Their businesses perpetuated a relationship established in the Ukraine between Jewish merchants and Russian Germans.[42]

The progression from cooperative farming to urban leadership followed by Joseph Nudelman and others has been overlooked in western Jewish history for several reasons. First, the continued dominance of Germans in western American Jewish communities well into the twentieth century has led historians to neglect the role of eastern Europeans. Second, because western agricultural colonies were generally considered failures, most of the historical literature on them tends to focus on explaining that failure. Finally, because most histories of these settlements are based on accounts left by the sponsors, they concentrate on the sponsors' roles and tend to obscure both the efforts of individual settlers and their lives after leaving the settlements. As a result, little attention has been paid to legacies of these settlements for western Jewish communities.

Studying the short-lived colony experiences as a chapter within the longer histories of the region, and of the colony families, allows for an appreciation of the contributions of these settlements. Despite their failure as colonies, these settlements helped shape a group of leaders who made significant contributions to Jewish communities in Portland and other western urban areas. In addition, colony experiments created migration streams of eastern European Jews to the rural West that continued after the settlements' demise.

NOTES

1. New Odessa Community Articles of Incorporation, 1883, Douglas County Courthouse, Roseburg, Oregon.

2. Details on the life of Joseph Nudelman come from Eugene R. Nudelman, *The Family of Joseph Nudelman* (self-published, 1969), and from an oral history of Eugene Nudelman taken by Shirley Nudelman as part of the Shirley Tanzer Oral History Project, Oregon Jewish Museum.

3. On the Am Olam, see Abraham Menes, "The *Am Oylom* Movement," *YIVO Annual of Jewish Social Science* 4 (1949), and Ellen Eisenberg, *Jewish Agricultural Colonies in New Jersey, 1882–1920* (Syracuse: Syracuse University Press, 1995), chapter 2.

4. Menes, "The *Am Oylom* Movement," 26–27.

5. Ibid., 24.

6. New Odessa Community, Articles of Incorporation.

7. Menes, "The *Am Oylom* Movement," 26–27.

8. Ibid., 29–30.

9. W. Gunther Plaut, "Jewish Colonies at Painted Woods and Devils Lake," *North Dakota History* 32 (1965): 62.

10. Mary Ann Barnes Williams, *Pioneer Days of Washburn, North Dakota, and Vicinity* (1936; reprint, McLean County Historical Society, 1995), 20.

11. Ibid., 21.

12. Nudelman, *Family of Joseph Nudelman*, 8.

13. Williams, *Pioneer Days*, 109.

14. Nudelman, *Family of Joseph Nudelman*, 9.

15. Robert Goldberg, "Zion in Utah: The Clarion Colony and Jewish Agrarianism," in *Jews of the American West*, ed. Moses Rischin and John Livingston (Detroit: Wayne State University Press, 1991).

16. Eisenberg, *Jewish Agricultural Colonies*, chapter 3.

17. On the Beersheba colony, see Lipman Goldman Feld, "New Light on the Lost Jewish Colony of Beersheba, Kansas, 1882–1886," *American Jewish Historical Quarterly* 60 (1970): 159–68.

18. Lois Fields Schwartz, "Early Jewish Agricultural Colonies in North Dakota," *North Dakota History* 32 (1965): 222; Plaut, "Jewish Colonies," 59–61.

19. Norton Stern, "The Orangevale and Porterville, California, Jewish Farm Colonies," *Western States Jewish Historical Quarterly* 10 (1978): 162.

20. Ibid., 163.

21. Norton Stern and William Kramer, "An American Zion in Nevada: The Rise and Fall of an Agricultural Colony," *Western States Jewish Historical Quarterly* 13, no. 2 (1981): 130–34.

22. See Ellen Eisenberg, "Transplanted to the Rose City: The Creation of an East European Jewish Community in Portland, Oregon," *Journal of American Ethnic History* 19 (2000): 82–97.

23. William Toll, *The Making of an Ethnic Middle Class: Portland Jewry over Four Generations* (Albany: State University of New York Press, 1982), 103.

24. Deborah Goldberg, "Jewish Spirit on the Urban Frontier" (undergraduate thesis, Reed College, 1982), 81.

25. Toll, *Making of an Ethnic Middle Class*, 103.

26. Goldberg, "Jewish Spirit on the Urban Frontier," 81.

27. Toll, *Making of an Ethnic Middle Class*, 101.

28. William C. Sherman et al., *Plains Folk: North Dakota's Ethnic History* (Fargo: North Dakota Institute for Regional Studies, 1986), 389–90.

29. Ibid., 400.

30. Federal Writers Project interviews, 1938, State Historical Society of North Dakota, Bismarck.

31. Feld, "New Light on the Lost Jewish Colony," 167–68.

32. J. Sanford Rikoon, ed., *Rachel Calof's Story: Jewish Homesteader on the Northern Plains* (Bloomington: Indiana University Press, 1995), 39–40.

33. Isadore Papermaster, "A History of North Dakota Jewry and Their Pioneer Rabbi," part 2, *Western States Jewish Historical Quarterly* 10, no. 2 (1978): 170.

34. Rikoon, *Rachel Calof's Story*, 119.

35. Schwartz, "Early Jewish Agricultural Colonies," 225–26.

36. Linda Mack Schloff, *"And Prairie Dogs Weren't Kosher": Jewish Women in the Upper Midwest since 1855* (St. Paul: Minnesota Historical Society, 1996), 116.

37. Plaut, "Jewish Colonies," 101.

38. Sherman, *Plains Folk*, 390.

39. Ibid., 391.

40. Ibid., 394.

41. Isadore Papermaster, "A History of North Dakota Jewry and Their Pioneer Rabbi," part 1, *Western States Jewish Historical Quarterly* 10, no. 1 (1977): 80.

42. Sherman, *Plains Folk*, 398–99.

Afterword

Moses Rischin

THE MANDATE OF the Autry Museum of Western Heritage, this historian was happily impressed to learn, is to pursue the exacting charge called for by its founder. That charge was to divest the history of the American West of its bunkum and hokum. That injunction came from Gene Autry, perhaps the world's most renowned singing cowboy of film, radio, and television. For three decades and more, Mr. Autry personified American individualism at its most romantic. Yet clearly, the Autry Museum, by its very name not the Gene Autry Museum, has alerted the new historians of the West that they were being welcomed if not quite to debunk the Gene Autry West then to write western history that would do honor to the historian's craft and allay the wide public craving for authentic history and genuine self-knowledge.

The historians contributing to *Jewish Life in the American West* have long been committed to supplanting unknowingness with knowingness, legend, myth, and hearsay with imaginatively researched, newly mined factuality, an enhanced sense of human complexity, and their own special perspectives. In these essays, the contributors have brought into bold relief some aspect of the distinctive ethnic and religious consciousness and individuality associated with new lives and old that Jewish newcomers assumed on coming west. In so doing, they have strived to relate the living West, its diverse Jews, and their various neighbors to one another so that all of us will better understand ourselves.

Sutter Street Temple of Congregation Emanu-El, San Francisco, dedicated on 23 March 1866. Courtesy of the Magnes Museum, Berkeley and San Francisco.

Front page of Ku Klux Klan brochure on restriction of immigration. Autry Museum of Western Heritage, Los Angeles.

Clearly the West, as place name, as place on the map, or as a vision in the public mind, has varied immensely from generation to generation. For that reason the contributors to this volume were encouraged to stake out their own lines of latitude and longitude. After crossing the Appalachians, the prairies, the Mississippi, and the ninety-eighth meridian, the West was to vault over the Great Divide onto the Pacific slope, with a latter-day welcome for good measure to Alaska and Hawaii, admitted as full-fledged states just after the mid-twentieth century and so completing the fifty United States of America.

Each stage in the ultimate continentalization of the United States led to a repositioning of the principals, the latest wave of settlers seeing themselves as the most western of westerners and the most emphatically American as they were farthest away from Europe. If the contributors to this volume have not presumed to quite encompass the western story geographically, it is because they have written history and not physical geography. Yet they do reflect in their perceptions and register in their nomenclature the immensity of the regional fervor generated in the westernizing of so much of the nation.

The contributors to this volume focus on Jewish settlement in the American West during the era of the Great Migration from the 1840s to the 1920s. Coming almost entirely from Europe, that North Atlantic migration was to be the greatest and most compressed transoceanic and transcontinental epic of population transference in world history, brought to an abrupt close only by the restrictive immigration law of 1924. After that statute was rescinded four decades later, immigration, progressively ever more Hispanic and Asian, once again has come to play a major role in every aspect of American life. Leading the way, of course, is California, the first state in the nation in population, immigration, and much else.

Not surprisingly, in the first half of the twentieth century, historians of the West and immigration historians alike were disinclined to recognize the integral relationship between the settlement of the West and its Euro-ethnic dimensions. Only with the concerted struggle by the United States during World War II to extend the blessings of the Four Freedoms to the whole world was the way opened to a pluralistic redefinition of American society. The 1960s particularly would promise to bring the full blessings of democracy to all Americans, whatever their origin, no less than to the latest newcomers from abroad.

Yet new western historians, who so intently incorporated the heretofore invisible histories of Native American peoples along with African and Asian Americans into the American canon, have been remiss in portraying

Russian passport and document with Dolinsky family portrait, which includes Nechama (Mollie) Dolinsky Goldberg, her father, and two brothers. Courtesy of the Beck Memorial Archives of Rocky Mountain Jewish History, Center for Judaic Studies and Penrose Library, University of Denver.

the varied experiences and distinctive relations to one another of the diverse Euro-ethnics who once flocked to the region in such great numbers. Their absence from most histories of the American West has continued to leave us without a deeper sense of the region's rich, if often equivocal, social and cultural complexity, including a better understanding of the roles that Jews came to play in responding to the need to fashion new etiquettes and codes of individual and group reciprocality.

In the introduction, Ava F. Kahn has provided the reader with a spirited overview of the Jewish experience in the American West from the 1840s to the 1920s, giving special attention to San Francisco, the region's stellar metropolis, and to California, where "the West has come to focus," as Earl Pomeroy has reminded us. From Kahn's California vantage point, Jews of the American West envisaged the region as their promised land. There, particularly, with little difficulty, they found a new equilibrium that fulfilled their aspirations as Americans and as Jews.

Congregation B'nai B'rith and various churches, Los Angeles, 1885. From the Archives of *Western States Jewish History*.

Hasia Diner sees the West from a decidedly different prospect. In the first essay, "American West, New York Jewish," she has utilized a comparative perspective that a bicoastal historian such as this one cannot help but find apposite, personally arresting, and provocative. Diner persuasively argues that American Jews as portrayed in the last half-century in the mass-media and in American Jewish historical scholarship have been captive to the prevailing bipolar rhetoric of American national identity. In that dialectic, the image of the ultra-American West, with its Jewish pioneers already innately Americans in the making in their every impulse and gesture, trumps the problematically American ultra-immigrant and New York Jewish image portrayed in the films, cartoons, and texts that Diner singles out for illustration. To this enigma, American Jews have, according to Diner, responded creatively. In their profound need to reify both their love for America and their love for their millennial-long Jewish religious tradition, they have opted for "American West, New York Jewish," and so they have been able to have it both ways. With a million Californians identified as Jews in the year 2001, and Berkeley's historic Judah L. Magnes Museum now joined to San Francisco's Jewish Museum, the Diner paradigm may be warmly contested by western Jews with a counterparadigm of their own, as may New York Jews of similar cast of mind with an equally confluent sense of their American Jewish identity.

In her essay "To Journey West: Jewish Women and Their Pioneer Stories," Ava F. Kahn turns to the close-up. Based on extant records in their own voices, she documents the roles played by four strikingly different women. Fanny Brooks in Utah, Mary Goldsmith Prag, chiefly in California, Flora Langermann Spiegelberg in New Mexico, and the long-suffering Leah Landman, primarily in Wyoming, each projected a singular resilience that was inseparable from the determination of each to leave a testament bearing witness to her trials and triumphs. Regrettably, less-gifted and less-fortunate women were without the resources to do so.

Treating another segment of the western story, "The Jewish Merchant and Civic Order in the Urban West," William Toll, one of the most erudite of American social historians, masterfully argues that many Jewish men acquired a civic stature and political weight in the West unmatched by successful Jewish frontier merchants in any other far-flung frontier society of the world. Yet in the early twentieth century, the corporate transformation of urban America subverted Main Street. In the American West, as elsewhere, the new scale of business promoted social stratification and geographic partitioning. The halcyon era of the small-town Jewish merchant was about to close but not before it left a profound mark.

While a Jewish merchant elite for a time largely fulfilled the exceptional promise of the urban frontier West, efforts by Russian Jewish immigrants to settle on the land have been written off by historians as doomed to failure from the outset. After being barred for centuries from landholding in Europe and peremptorily crowded into urban slums in America's industrializing cities, many Jewish immigrants were determined, no matter what the cost, to transform themselves into farmers. Bethlehem Yehudah, South Dakota; Painted Woods, North Dakota; Beersheba, Kansas; Cotopaxi, Colorado; and New Odessa, Oregon, were among the dozen short-lived colonies that Jewish immigrants founded in the West from the 1880s to the early years of the twentieth century.

In her pathbreaking essay, "From Cooperative Farming to Urban Leadership," Ellen Eisenberg focuses not on the failed colonists to whom Robert A. Goldberg of the University of Utah has recently paid such eloquent tribute but on the subsequent lives of the failed persisters. The richly informative family account of the Joseph Nudelman clan, especially, has enabled Eisenberg to demonstrate Nudelman's devotion to the colony ideal and the agrarian vision and to document his urban leadership abilities, remarkable adaptive skills, and passion for Jewish institution building in Portland. The success of the persisters after their initial failure also brought to states like North Dakota a corps of hundreds of additional Jewish immigrants who possessed special gifts for the fostering of a vital western society with a sense of communalism inspired by their agrarian venture.

Each of these original and suggestive historical essays brings us ever closer to an understanding of the western Jewish experience and opens the way to further inquiry and exploration.

Selected Readings

This list of resources, a supplement to the works referred to in the notes, is provided in order to assist readers in learning more about western Jewish history, a new and thriving field. While several of the books are out of print, most can be found in libraries. Interested readers may also wish to consult *Western States Jewish History* (formerly *Western States Jewish Historical Quarterly*) and the publications of the Southern California Jewish Historical Society and other local Jewish historical associations.

Auerbach, Samuel H. *Utah Pioneer Merchant: The Memories of Samuel H. Auerbach, 1847–1920*. Berkeley: University of California, Berkeley, Bancroft Library, 1998.

Benjamin, I. J. *Three Years in America, 1859–1862*. Philadelphia: The Jewish Publication Society of America, 1956.

Breck, Allen D. *A Centennial History of the Jews of Colorado, 1859–1959*. Denver: The Hirschfeld Press, 1960.

Calof, Rachel. *Rachel Calof's Story: Jewish Homesteader on the Northern Plains*. Edited by J. Sanford Rikoon, translated by Jacob Calof and Molly Shaw. Bloomington: Indiana University Press, 1995.

Cogan, Sara G. *The Jews of Los Angeles 1849–1945: An Annotated Bibliography*. Berkeley: Western Jewish History Center of the Judah L. Magnes Museum, 1980.

———. *The Jews of San Francisco and the Greater Bay Area 1849–1919: An Annotated Bibliography*. Berkeley: Western Jewish History Center of the Judah L. Magnes Museum, 1973.

———. *Pioneer Jews of the California Mother Lode, 1849–1880: An Annotated Bibliography*. Berkeley: Western Jewish History Center of the Judah L. Magnes Museum, 1968.

Coleman, Julie L. *Golden Opportunities: A Biographical History of Montana's Jewish Communities*. Billings, Mont.: Falcon Press, 1994.

Cristol, Gerry. *A Light in the Prairie: Temple Emanu-El of Dallas 1872–1997*. Fort Worth: Texas Christian University Press, 1998.

D'Ancona, David A. *A California-Nevada Travel Diary of 1876: The Delightful Account of a Ben B'rith*. Edited by William M. Kramer. Santa Monica: Norton B. Stern Publisher, 1975.

Dinnerstein, Leonard. *Antisemitism in America*. New York: Oxford University Press, 1994.

Dinnerstein, Leonard, and Mary Dale Palsson, eds. *Jews in the South*. Baton Rouge: Louisiana State University Press,1973.

Eisenberg, Ellen. *Jewish Agricultural Colonies in New Jersey 1882–1920*. New York: Syracuse University Press, 1995.

Glanz, Rudolf. *The Jews in American Alaska, 1867–1880*. New York: H. H. Glanz, 1953.

————.*The Jews of California, from the Discovery of Gold until 1880*. New York and Los Angeles: Southern California Jewish Historical Society, 1960.

Glazier, Jack. *Dispersing the Ghetto: The Relocation of the Jewish Immigrants across America*. Ithaca: Cornell University Press, 1998.

Hersher, Uri D. *Jewish Agricultural Utopias in America, 1880–1910*. Detroit: Wayne State University Press, 1981.

Korn, Bertram Wallace. *Travels and Adventures in the Far West, by Solomon Nunes Carvalho*. Philadelphia: The Jewish Publication Society of America, 1954.

Kramer, William M., ed. *The Western Journal of Isaac Mayer Wise,1877*. Berkeley: Western Jewish History Center, Magnes Museum, 1974.

Levinson, Robert E. *The Jews in the California Gold Rush*. Berkeley: Commission for the Preservation of Pioneer Jewish Cemeteries and Landmarks of the Judah L. Magnes Museum, 1994.

Litman, Simon. *Ray Frank Litman: A Memoir*. New York: American Jewish Historical Society, 1957.

Lowenstein, Steven. *The Jews of Oregon, 1850–1950*. Portland: Jewish Historical Society of Oregon, 1987.

Meyer, Martin A. *Western Jewry: An Account of the Achievements of the Jews and Judaism in California, Including Eulogies and Biographies*. San Francisco: Emanu-El, 1916 (reissued 2001).

Narell, Irena. *Our City: The Jews of San Francisco*. San Diego: Howell-North Books, 1981.

Rockaway, Robert A. *Words of the Uprooted: Jewish Immigrants in Early Twentieth-Century America*. Ithaca: Cornell University Press, 1998.

Rosenbaum, Fred. *Free to Choose: The Making of a Jewish Community in the American West*. Berkeley: Judah L. Magnes Memorial Museum, 1976.

————. *Visions of Reform: Congregation Emanu-El and the Jews of San Francisco, 1849–1999*. Berkeley: Judah L. Magnes Museum, 2000.

Shapiro,Amy. *A Guide to the Jewish Rockies, Colorado, Montana, Wyoming*. Denver: Rocky Mountain Jewish Historical Society, Center for Judaic Studies, University of Denver, 1979.

Stern, Norton B. *California Jewish History: A Descriptive Bibliography—over five hundred fifty works for the period Gold Rush to post–World War I*. Glendale: A. H. Clark Co., 1967.

Tobias, Henry Jack. *A History of the Jews in New Mexico*. Albuquerque: University of New Mexico Press, 1990.

————. *The Jews in Oklahoma*. Norman: University of Oklahoma Press, 1980.

Toll, William. *The Making of an Ethnic Middle Class: Portland Jewry over Four Generations*. Albany: State University of New York Press, 1982.

Uchill, Ida Libert. *Pioneers, Peddlers, and Tsadikim: The Story of Jews in Colorado*. Boulder: University of Colorado Press, 2000.

Voorsanger, Jacob. *The Chronicles of Emanu-El: Being an Account of the Rise and Progress of the Congregation Emanu-El*. San Francisco: Emanu-El, 1900.

Vorspan, Max, and Lloyd P. Gartner. *History of the Jews of Los Angeles*. San Marino, Calif.: Huntington Library, 1970.

Watters, Leon L. *The Pioneer Jews of Utah*. New York: American Jewish Historical Society, 1952.

Acknowledgments

The Autry Museum of Western Heritage first began to develop this volume and the related traveling exhibition with the advice and encouragement of Board Treasurer Stanley Schneider. Founding President and Chief Executive Officer Joanne D. Hale and her successor, John L. Gray, made certain that museum staff members were motivated and had necessary resources to complete their tasks. A sometimes feisty project team deserves special thanks; Sergio Aguilera, Jeffrey Barber, David Burton, Evelyn Davis, Clyde Derrick, Michael Duchemin, Marva Felchlin, Laurie German, Meredith Hackelman, Suzanne Haddad, Chris Keledjian, Mark Lewis, Lisa Marr, Joan Marshall, Sandra Odor, Linda Strauss, Emily Wolfson, and Susan Van De Vyvere all made realization of the exhibition possible.

Our advisory committee deserves grateful appreciation. Among those we would like to thank personally are Susan Morris, director of the Magnes Museum; Harriet Rochlin, pioneering historian of pioneer Jews in the West; Dr. William Kramer, rabbi and author, who helped create the field; Adele Burke and Grace Grossman, colleagues at the Skirball Museum; Gladys Sturman and David Epstein, publisher and editor of *Western States Jewish History*; Dr. Barry Glassner, director of the Casden Institute for the Study of the Jewish Role in American Life, University of Southern California (USC); and David Schoulder, president of the New Mexico Jewish Historical Society. Community leaders on the committee have been most supportive and include Lionel and Terry Bell; Lloyd B. Dennis; Irwin Field; Rabbi Harvey J. Fields, Ph.D.; Jona Goldrich; Mr. and Mrs. Osias Goren; Steven Gunther; Joanne D. Hale; Michael A. Hirschfeld, executive director, Jewish Community Relations Committee, the Jewish Federation; Dr. Selma Holo, director, Fisher Gallery, USC; Rachel Levin; Jerry Magnin; Larry Ramer; Susan Robertson; Stephen Sass; Stan Schneider; Nathan Shapell; Annette Shapiro; John Sussman; and Larry Weinberg.

A special acknowledgment for funding this project goes to the following individuals, foundations, and companies: Wells Fargo, the Righteous Persons Foundation, the Walter and Elise Haas Fund, the Maurice Amado Foundation, the Plum Foundation, the David and Fela Shapell Foundation, and the Western States Jewish History Association.

Ava Kahn expresses personal thanks to Moses Rischin, Ruth Haber, and Mitchell Richman, who kindly commented on drafts of her work, and to James Nottage, who asked her to join him in this pioneering venture.

JAMES NOTTAGE and AVA F. KAHN, PH.D.
Indianapolis and Berkeley

Index

Page numbers in **bold** refer to illustrations.

acculturation, 16, 18
Acoma Pueblo, 8, 103–4
activism, women's, 66–67
African Americans, 41
Ahavai Shalom, Portland, 125
Alaska Commercial Company, 92, 94, 104
Alaska, settlement in, 21
Albany, Oregon, 28, 83, 92, 93, 95, 98
Am Olam movement, 42, 115–17, 129
America, as promised land, 13, 14, 29, 53
American Jewish Historical Society, 39–40
American Tail, An, 33, 36
Americanization, 16, 18, 126–27
anti-Semitism, 107, 117, 121
Arizona, 18, 28, 29, 40, 83, 103, 104
artisans, 83, 93
Ashkenazi communities, 8
Auerbach, Eveline Brooks, 55, **56**, 58
August, Jennie, 9
Auraria, Colorado, 21
Austria-Hungary, immigrants from, 47

Baker, Oregon, 89
Bamberger, Simon, 21
Baron de Hirsch Fund, 45
Bavaria, immigrants from, 19
Beersheba colony, 121–22, 127
benevolent societies, 19, 58, 100
Benjamin, I. J., 100
Bergman, Andy, 37
Beth Israel, Portland, 100
Bethlehem Judea, South Dakota, 115–16, 117, 121, 128
Bibo, Solomon, 7–**8**, 103–4
Bitterman, Simon, 9
Blazing Saddles, 37
B'nai Abraham, 106

B'nai B'rith, 46, 101–2, 103, 106
B'nai Israel, Salt Lake City, 21, 48
Boise, Idaho, 60
Boyle Heights, Los Angeles, 40
Breed Street shul, Los Angeles, 40
Breslau, Prussia, immigrants from, 57
Brooks Arcade, Salt Lake City, **61**
Brooks, Fanny, 53, 54, 55–62; **56**, 76
Brooks, Julius Gerson, 57–61
Brooks, Max, 58
Brooks, Mel, 36
Brown, Benjamin, 120
burial grounds, 19
Burns, Oregon, 89, 90
business practices, 88–89, 91

California, 19, 21, 23, 24, 40, 53; collective farming in, 114, 119–20
California State Teachers' Association, 66
Calof, Abraham, **126**
Calof, Rachel Bella, **126**, 127–28
Calof, Rachel Kahn, 113
Cantor, Eddie, 37
Canyon City, Oregon, 89
Carson City, Nevada, 98
Catholic-Jewish relations, 70
Cedar Rapids, Iowa, 46
cemetery associations, 100
Central City, Colorado, 21
central European Jews, and the West, 39, 47–49
Centralia, Washington, 98
Cerf, Clothilde, 9
Chehalis, Washington, 98
Chicago, 40, 44, 45, 46
children, 9, 46, 95–96
Chinese Americans, 41
civic boosters, 100–101

Clarion Colony, Utah, 116, 120–21
Cleveland, Ohio, 46
Clovillaud, Mary Murphy, 58
Cohen, Charlie, 74
Cohen, David Solis, 103
Cohen, Rabbi Henry, **27**, 46
Cohn, Adolph, 93
Cohn, Bernard, 93
Cohn, Henry, 18
Cohn, Isadore, 93
Cohn, Kaspare, 14, 93
Cohn, Ray (Mrs. Ben Meyer), **14**
Colorado, 18, 21, 23, 40; collective farming in, 114
Columbia, California, 18
community building, 97–100
Congregation Aaron, Trinidad, Colorado, 101, **102**
Congregation B'nai B'rith, Los Angeles, **136**
Congregation Emanuel, Denver, 21
Congregation Montefiore, Salt Lake City, 48
Congregation Neveh Zedek, 124
Congregation Talmud Torah, Portland, 125
Connecticut Daughters of the American Revolution, 34
cooperative farming, 113–30
Cotopaxi, Colorado, 116
Covenant House, 48
Cremieux, South Dakota, 116, 128
Cronon, William, 90

Dallas, Texas, 25
Davis, Jacob, 49
Democratic Club of San Francisco, 9
Denver, Colorado, 18, 21, 25, 43–44, 46, 48
Denver Sheltering Home for Jewish Children, **17**
department stores, rise of, 105–6
Devils Lake, North Dakota, 113, 115, 126, 127–28
Diner, Hasia R., 101
Dixon, California, 9
Dolinsky family, **135**
Downey, John G., 84
Durkheimer, Julius, 105
Durkheimer, Sylvan, 88

eastern European Jews, and the West, 39, 47–49, 114
Eckman, Julius, 64
Edelman, Isak, 127
education, 62, 66–67, 74

Ellensburg, Washington, 94, 95
Emanu-El, Temple, San Francisco, 18, 19, 66, 100, **132**
Emes, Der (newspaper), 49
employment, categories of, 92–94
England, immigrants from, 19, 25
Eugene, Oregon, 90
Europe, Jewish communities in, 14; return to, 88
European migratory patterns, 85–86

family networks, 92–94
Farmers & Merchants Bank, 84, 99
farming, 24; cooperative, 113–30
Fievel Goes West, 36, 38
films, 33, 36–37
Fleishackers, 92
Florence, Nebraska, 57
Frankel, Adolph, **12**
Frankel, Sam, **12**
Frey, William, **112**, 117, 121
Friedlander, Samuel, 102
Friedman, Sara, 9
Friendly, Seymour, 90, 95
Frisco Kid, 37, 38
fur trade, 92

Gale, Marcus, 124
Galena, Illinois, 57
Galveston Movement (or Plan), 22–23, 45–46
Galveston, Texas, 13, 17, 27
garment industry, 49–51
Gatzert, Bailey, 84
Germany, immigrants from, 25
gold rush, Alaska, 21
gold rush, California, 19, 47, 54, 57, 83, 88
Goldsmith, Bernard, 87–88, 105
Goldsmith, Isaac, 62, **64**
Goldsmith, Sarah, 62, **64**
Goldwater, Michael, 18
Goldwater, Morris, 103
Gradwohl, Julius and Elvira, 93
Grand Forks, North Dakota, 127
Greenberg, Ben Zion, 127

Hamburger, Moses, 105
Hamburger's department store, Los Angeles, 107
Haskalah, 115
Hebrew Benevolent Society, 58
Hellman, H. M., 88
Hellman, I. W., 84

Hirsch, Harold, 107
Hirsch, Solomon, 103
historians, and western Jewish history, 16, 39–42, 133–37
Holland, 86
Homestead Act, 116, 121
homesteading, 24, 72–73, 116, 121
"Hominy's famous Jewish champion of the lariat & saddle," **6**
How We Lived, 42
Howe, Irving, 42
Hungary, immigrants from, **12**–13
Huntington, Henry, 84

I. Magnin & Company, 107
immigration, rates of, 14
Immigration Restriction Act, 26
Industrial Removal Office (I.R.O.), 45–46, 47
infant mortality, 96
institutions, Jewish, creation of, 48
Iowa, settlement in, 23
Irish Americans, 41
Isaacs, Carrie Newmark, **10**
Isaacs, J. L., **10**, 11
Italian Americans, 41

Jacobs, Frances Wisebart, 46
Jacoby Brothers, Los Angeles, California, **97**
jeans, 49
Jewish Agricultural Society, 73
Jewish Consumptives Relief Society, 46
Jewish Immigration Information Bureau, 27, 46
Jewish Museum, San Francisco, 136
Jewish People in America, The, 39–40
Jewish Theatrical Company, **43**
Jews of the American West, 16
Jews, origins of American, 8
Jonas, Marcus, 11

Kahn, Florence Prag, 65, 76
Kahn, Julius, 13, 19, **22**, 29
Kansas, settlement in, 23; collective farming in, 114, 116, 121
Katz, George, 9
Katz, Hartz Naftel, 127
Katzenogy, Joseph, 49
Kishinev Pogrom, 14
Kleinberg, Amelia, 94–95
Kleinberg, Henry, 94–95
Korrick's New York store, 18, **23**
Kremenchug, Russia, 115
Ku Klux Klan, **134**

Labbatt, Henry, 100
Ladies Hebrew Benevolent Society, 90
land ownership, 17, 113–30
Landman, Leah, 53, 54, 55, 71–76
Landman, Minnie, 53, 55, 73–76
Landman, Simon, 71–76
Langermann, William, 68
leadership, community, 18, 66–67, 68, 103–4
Leadville, Colorado, 11, 21
Levi, Leo N., 45
Levi Strauss & Co., **82**, 92
Levin, Max, 125
Levison, Alice Gerstle, 94
Levite, Abraham, **15**
Levite, William, **15**
Levy, Benish, 91
Levy, Harriet Lane, 53, 85, 94, 100
Levy, Rabbi Leonard, 73
Lewis, Philip, 94, 105
Libo, Kenneth, 42
Lilienthal, Philip, 123
Lipman, Isaac, 105
Lithuania, immigrants from, 25, 47
Loeb, Estelle Newmark, **89**
Loeb, Rose, **89**
London, England, 71–72
Longview, Washington, 98
Los Angeles, settlement in, 21, 25, **26, 36,** 40,
    44, 49; merchants in, 87, 94, 98–99, **136**
Lowenstein, Steven, 43
Lower East Side, New York, **32,** 40

Magnes Museum, Berkeley, 136
map, U.S. (Yiddish), **34–35**
marketing networks, 98–99
marriage 22, 93–97
Marysville, California, 58
Masonry, 101, 102–3
Meier, Jeanette Hirsch, 92
merchandising, circular, 87
merchants, 18, 58, 83–107
Mexicans, and Jewish merchants, 98–99
Meyer, Jacob, 100
Midwest, women and, 53
migration, and women, 54–55
migration, chains, 22, 85, 86; serial, 78; step, 16
migratory patterns, Jewish, 85–86
millinery, 60, 61
mining rushes, 18, 19–21
Minnesota, collective farming in, 114
Montana, settlement in, 40

Mormons, relationships with, 58, 65
multiethnic communities, 57–58, 76–77

Nathan, Sarah, 18
national character, and Jewishness, 37–38
National Home for Asthmatic Children, 17
National Jewish Hospital, 17
National Jewish Hospital for Consumptives, 46
Nebraska, settlement in, 23
Nevada, settlement in, 21; collective farming
    in, 123
New Mexico, settlement in, 22, 40, 55
New Odessa, Oregon, 25, 42, 113, 116, 117,
    121
New York Dry Goods Store, 18
New York, locus of American Jewish experi-
    ence, 13, 16, 33, 37, 39, 40–50
Newmark Block, Los Angeles, **26**
Newmark family, **10,** 88–92, **89**
Newmark, Ella, **10**
Newmark, Emily, **10**
Newmark, Harris, **10, 87,** 88–89, 90, 99
Newmark, Joseph, **89**
Newmark, Meyer J., **87**
Newmark, Sarah, **89**
North Dakota Development League, 128
North Dakota, settlement in, 23, 24, 53;
    collective farming in, 113, 115, 126, 127–128
Nudelman family, **119,** 123–24
Nudelman, Fanny, **120**
Nudelman, Joseph, 114–15, 117, 118–19, **120,**
    123

Oakland, California, 9
Odessa, Russia, immigrants from, 115, 117–20
Oklahoma City, settlements in, 46
Oklahoma, settlements in, 23, 46
Olympia, Washington, 98
Omaha, Nebraska, 25, 75
Orangevale, California, 120
Orangevale Stock Farm Association, 129
Oregon, settlements in, 21, 24, 40, 43
Orthodox Jews, 48

Painted Woods farming collective, 115, 117,
    118, 119, 120, 122–23, 128
Palace of the Governors, Santa Fe, **70**
Palm Theatre, Denver, 43
Papermaster, Rabbi Benjamin, 128
Philadelphia, 40, 44
Phoenix, Arizona, 18, 23
Picon, Molly, 44–45

Pioneer Jews: A New Life in the Far West, 39
pogroms, 14
Poland, immigrants from, 19, 25, 37, 55, 62
Policar family, **20**
Popper, Carlotta, 61
Porterville, California, 119–20
Portland, Oregon, settlers in, 21, 25, 43, 48,
    49, 60; merchant activity in, 88, 90, 92, 98,
    103; community leadership, 120, 124
Portugal, A., 88
Posen, immigration from, 47, 64
Prag, Conrad, 64–67
Prag, Mary Goldsmith, 53, 55, 62–67, **63,** 76
Prager, Regina, 49
Prager, Sam, 99
Prairie City, Oregon, 89, 90
Prescott, Arizona, 28, 83
press, Yiddish, 44, 49
Prussia, immigrants from, 25, 47, 54
Puget Sound National Bank, 84

railroads, 78, 85, 86, 88, 98–99
Raphael Weil & Company, 107
Reform movement, 48
Reno, Nevada, 94, 98
Rhodes, immigrants from, 25
Rischin, Moses, 16, 29
rituals, 100
Rochlin, Fred, 39
Rochlin, Harriet, 39
Roseburg, Oregon, 113
Rosenthal, Herman, 116
Roth family, **28, 29**
Russia, immigrants from, 19, 25, 37, 71, 73,
    113–30

Sabbath Visitor, 8
Sack, Samuel, **116**
Sacramento, 88
Salinger family, 93
Salt Lake City, settlers in, 48, 54, 58, 60–62,
    65–67
San Diego, California, 21
San Francisco, **59;** settlers in, 9, 18, 25, **38,**
    44, 48, 53, 54, merchants in, 64, 68, 91, 92;
    migration from, 19; and Yiddish culture, 48–
    49
Sands Brothers, Helena, MT, **84**
Santa Fe, New Mexico, 22, 68–71, 83
Santa Fe Trail, 22, 55, 68
Schiff, Jacob, 22, 45, 46, 114, 115
Schlissel, Lillian, 53

Schloff, Linda Mack, 53
Schwabacher & Company, 84
Schwartz, Philip, 18
Seattle, Washington, 21, 25, 48, 49; merchants in, 84, 98
Second National Bank of New Mexico, 69
Selling, Ben, 88, 90, 91, 103, 105, 106
Sephardic communities, 8, 19, 25, 106
Sephardic Congregations of Seattle, **30**
Shaarei Tzedek, Salt Lake City, 48
Shaarie Torah, Portland, 120
Sherith Israel temple, San Francisco, 18, 19, **25**, 64, **66**
shofar, **11**, 65
Sichel, Sig, 103
Simon, Joseph, 103, **104**
small towns, 21
social networks, 92–97
socialism, 115
Sorin, Gerald, 39–40, 43
South Dakota, settlement in, 24
Spiegelberg brothers, 22, **69**, 83
Spiegelberg, Flora Langermann, **52**, 53, 68–71, 76
Spiegelberg, Willi, 68–71, **69**, **70**
Spielberg, Steven, 33
Spivak, Dr. Charles, 46
Spring Hill Water Company, 84
stained-glass window, Congregation Sherith Israel, 25

Stenge, Laura, 9
Strauss, Charles, 104, **106**
Strauss, Levi, 49
suffrage, women's, 66
Swett, Zachary, 124–25
synagogues, 19, 100–101

Tacoma, Washington, 83, 98
tailors, 21
Temple Beth Israel, Portland, Oregon, 96
Temple Block, Los Angeles, **97**
Texas, settlement in, 22–23, 45
theater, Yiddish 44, 48–49
Timbuctoo, California, **55**, 59
Torrington, Wyoming, 72, 74
Trinidad, Colorado, 83
Trupin, Sophie, 53
Tucson, Arizona, 104
Tulare County, California, 119
Turner, Frederick Jackson, 45

union movement, 50
urban Jewish culture, 37–38
Utah, settlements in, 21, 40, 55; collective farming in, 114

Virginia City, Nevada, 83, 92, 94, 98, 99–100
Voorsanger, Rabbi, 123

Waldman, Morris, 46
Washington, settlement in, 21; marketing networks, 98
We Lived There, Too, 43
Wechsler Colony, **118**
Wechsler, Rabbi Judah, 118, 122–23
Wellington, Nevada, 119
Western experience, contrast with New York, 33, 34,
westerner, definition, 7
Whoopee!, 37
Wilder, Gene, 37
Willamette Valley, Oregon, 113
Wirth, Louis, 45
Wise, Rabbi Isaac Mayer, 121
Wolfe, Adolph, 103
women, 27, 53–79; Mormon, 65
World of Our Fathers, The, 42
Wymore Ranch, Nevada, 123
Wyoming, settlement in, 53, 55, 72–76

Yiddish culture, 48
Yiddish, map of U.S., **34–35**
Yiddisher Cowboy, Der, 37
Yiddisher Geist, Der (newspaper), 49
Yidisher Kauboy, Der, 37
Young, Brigham, 62, 65

Zionist movement, 24, 106, 115